HEAVY WEATHER CRUISING

HEAVY WEATHER CRUISING

Tom Cunliffe

INTERNATIONAL MARINE
PUBLISHING COMPANY
Camden, Maine 04843

Published by International Marine Publishing Company, a division of Highmark Publishing, Ltd., 21 Elm Street, Camden, Maine 04843
207-237-4837

First published in Great Britain by Fernhurst Books
Printed and bound in Great Britain
10 9 8 7 6 5 4 3 2 1

ISBN 0-87742-975-8

Acknowledgements

The publishers would like to thank the Westerley Sea School for the loan of a yacht for use in the photo sessions, and Tom Cunliffe and Christine Graves for sailing it. The material on yacht stability has been reproduced from the 1979 Fastnet Inquiry with the permission of the R.Y.A. and the R.O.R.C.

The cover design is by Behram Kapadia.

Photographs

The photographs are by John Woodward, with the exception of the following (indicated by page number):
Andrew Bray 31; John Etches 55; Peter Haward 39; William Payne 35 (top); R.K. Pilsbury 45; *Yachting Monthly* 15, 19, 22, 46, 50, 56.
The cover photograph is by Patrick Roach.

Design by John Woodward
Composition by A & G Phototypesetters, Knaphill
Artwork by PanTek, Maidstone
Printed by Hollen Street Press, Slough

Contents

Introduction

The object of this book is to help you to deal with all grades of foul weather, from the stiff blow that loses you one day of a summer cruise through to the storm that throws doubt on your ability to survive.

Every sailor is fascinated by the subject of heavy weather. There are probably more strongly-held opinions about how to cope with it than about any other question related to seafaring, but if you try to define it you soon discover that, like happiness, hard weather is different things to different people. An experienced crew in a 50-foot cutter sailing on a broad reach in a force six wind ought to be thoroughly enjoying themselves. In the same conditions a family group who have been working to windward for 24 hours in a 20-foot bilge keeler could well be near snapping point.

Heavy weather could be defined as any combination of wind and sea of sufficient severity to cause the crew of a particular boat to consider altering their plans. But weather at sea is capable of worsening far beyond that marginal situation, and sooner or later any boat may meet circumstances in which she can do little more than drift helplesly into mortal danger. The art of skippering is to so handle yourself, your crew and your boat that you steer clear of that final truth for a whole lifetime.

In order to do this you need a well-found yacht, a sound knowledge of the options available and a positive self-reliant approach.

The message throughout this book is one of self-help: keeping clear of trouble if you can, and dealing with it if you can't. You will find nothing between these covers that tells you how to call for help. A yacht can finish up in need of the Search and Rescue Services for many reasons, only one of which is foundering in a gale of wind. There are specialist publications available which explain how best to set about being rescued if you leave yourself with no alternative, but being rescued has nothing to do with the art of bad weather seamanship, the whole essence of which is to keep yourself clear of such situations. Sailing in heavy weather is an inevitable part of life on the water. It can be a nightmare, or it can provide that spice of real action which all yachtsmen secretly – or not so secretly – desire. The satisfaction of having organised your resources so as to come through a blow undamaged and without fuss is one of the greatest joys the sea has to offer.

The resources to achieve this result are there already. The following pages will help you to identify and draw on them at sea when the wind blows hard.

1 Wind and wave

Wind is what sailing is all about. Wind powers the rig which drives the boat along; wind heels the boat over; wind direction decides whether we beat or sail free; wind strength and direction are the weather predictions in which we are most interested. Wind also stirs up the surface of the sea and makes waves, and in the last analysis it is waves which are most likely to spoil our day.

Wind: the Beaufort Scale in perspective

If you listen to broadside folk ballads of the eighteenth century you will hear some strange weather reports. We are advised that when General Wolfe's men set sail 'the wind it blew a pleasant gale'. This sort of muddy concept of weather conditions became obsolete when Admiral Beaufort produced his famous scale of wind forces. Originally designed for use in Royal Navy ships it related wind speed to the sails a standard frigate or ship of the line would choose to set, all things being equal. His wind forces ran from 0-12 and so successful were his efforts that to this day most maritime nations refer to wind strength on the Beaufort Scale. Nowadays wind force is carefully quantified, but the average yachtsman, like Nelson's captains, is more concerned about what sail he can carry than whether the true wind is blowing at 15 or 17 knots.

Wind pressure

As wind speed increases, the pressure exerted by the flowing air rises at a dramatic rate. At 15 knots (force 4), it is 0.8 pounds per square foot. At 30 knots (force 7) it has quadrupled to 3.1 pounds per square foot, and by the time the heady figure of 60 knots comes along in a full hurricane-force blow, we are up to around 12.3 pounds. A ghastly shock awaits the inexperienced mariner who is under the impression that force 8 is twice as windy as force 4! Five times as bad is nearer the mark and, of course, that's only the wind. The real enemy is the sea.

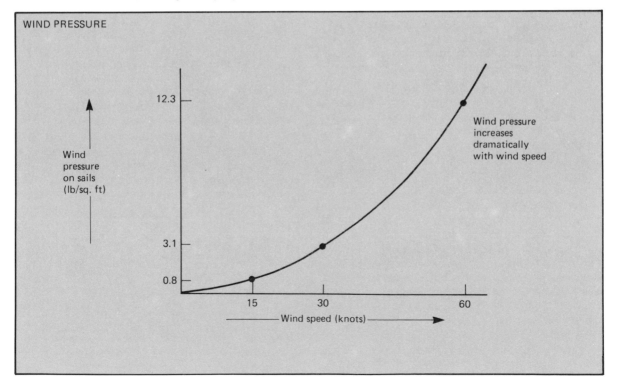

WIND PRESSURE

Wind pressure on sails (lb/sq. ft)

12.3

3.1

0.8

15   30   60

Wind speed (knots)

Wind pressure increases dramatically with wind speed

Gusts

All forecast wind strengths are given as *mean* wind speeds. A strong breeze officially described as being force 6 (22 – 27 knots) may, in fact, vary from 20 knots in the lulls to some evil gusts blasting up to 30. Twenty knots is force 5 on the Beaufort Scale, comfortably within the windward capacity of a small cruiser. Thirty knots is well into force 7, which is double the real wind force, and is quite capable of giving such a boat a very unpleasant afternoon.

In open water, different types of air mass will lead to more or less gusty conditions. The unstable polar maritime air that comes swishing down behind a cold front is high on the gustiness list whereas a stable 'tropical maritime' south-westerly breeze is likely to be a lot steadier.

Squalls

A squall is a local disturbance in the airstream which, in one form or another, produces conditions more violent than those currently being experienced.

You can usually see a squall coming because its presence is given away by a cloud effect. Squall clouds come in various shapes and sizes and will be discussed in Chapter 4. For now it is enough to understand that a bad squall can turn fifteen minutes of a fresh, windy day into a temporary horror show.

Local effects on a steady wind

A given surface wind blows more strongly over the sea than it does over land because water offers less frictional resistance to its passing. The presence of land also tends to break up the steady flow of air. These two factors mean that close to leeward of a coastline there is often a zone where the wind is lighter than it is offshore. However, certain types of land mass can cause accelerated wind speeds or eccentric wind directions.

Air funnelling down a valley to windward will frequently create a local increase in wind speed, while immediately to windward of a high land mass or a steep cliff there may be a zone of light or turbulent wind.

If the high land is the right shape, the wind may well be accelerated down the lee side, causing considerably increased gusting. In locations where particularly steep mountains coincide with narrow sea leads (such as the fjords of western Norway) some fearsome conditions of this type may be experienced. The Norwegians call this a 'falling wind'; as the author discovered to his cost, such terrible winds have a measurable downward component, and are no fun at all.

So don't assume you'll get a lee from land to weather of you. It may help the sea state, but its effect on the wind will be less predictable.

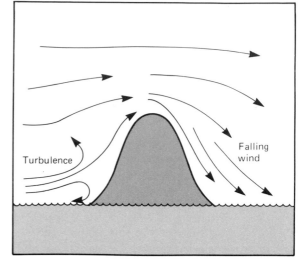

Above: High land can have dramatic effects on local wind conditions, with turbulence to windward and occasional 'falling winds' to leeward.

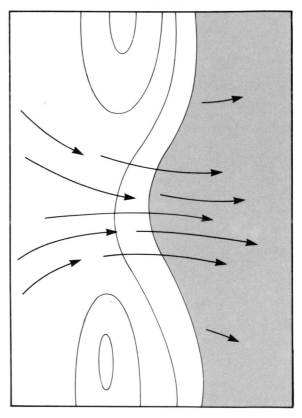

Above: Air blowing through a gap in the hills on a nearby coast will often cause a local increase in windspeed over the sea to leeward.

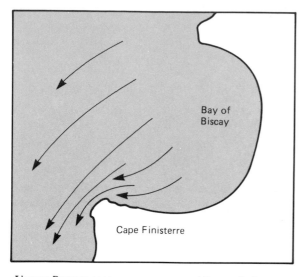

Above: Breezy corners may occur at the end of a continental landmass such as Cape Finisterre (left) or on a projecting headland (right).

True and apparent wind

An understanding of the difference between true and apparent wind is of particular importance in bad weather. True wind is the airstream experienced passively by a boat that is stationary. Once that boat starts moving through the water she moves through the air as well, and this has a direct effect on the wind blowing across her deck.

If a boat motors at six knots in still air, she receives a six-knot headwind. This is obviously apparent wind. Conversely if she motors downwind at six knots in a six-knot breeze, she would feel no wind at all: an apparent lack of wind. If she now turns and motors dead to windward at six knots in the same six-knot breeze, the wind will appear to blow at 12 knots.

There is, therefore, a 12-knot difference in the wind the boat actually experiences (the apparent wind) is she is travelling upwind or downwind. When the true wind is averaging 28 knots (the bottom end of force 7) a boat running before it at 6 knots will be enjoying a fine sailing breeze of 22 knots (force 5 or 6). If she turns upwind her apparent wind will increase to something approaching force 8, a whole gale. The pressure of the wind on a given sail area will double, and instead of running comfortably with the sea the boat will have to smash her way through every wave. She is in an entirely different world.

Right: Apparent wind is a combination of the true wind speed and the boat's speed; both the strength and direction of the apparent wind are affected.

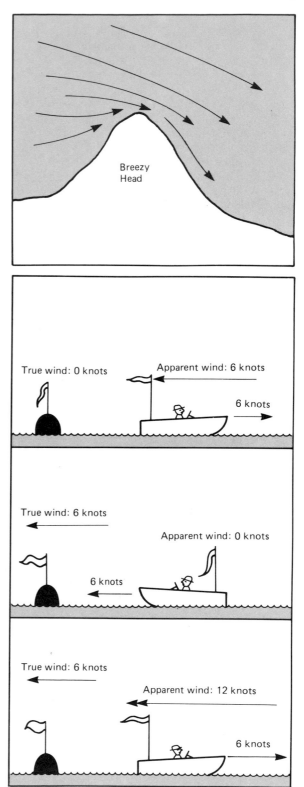

A yachtsman's Beaufort Scale

WIND FORCE	WIND SPEED	DESCRIPTION	PROBABLE WAVE HEIGHT		TYPICAL BOATS – WIND FORWARD OF THE BEAM		
			MIN.	MAX.	20' BILGE KEELER	32' MODERATE C/RACER	50' HEAVY DISP. CRUISER
0	0-1 KNOT	CALM	0 FEET	0 FEET	MOTORING	MOTORING	MOTORING
1	1-3	LIGHT AIR	0	0	MOTORING	MOTORING	MOTORING
2	4-6	LIGHT BREEZE	0.1	0.3	GENOA AND FULL MAIN	GENOA AND FULL MAIN	GENOA AND FULL MAIN
3	7-10	GENTLE BREEZE	0.4	1	GENOA AND FULL MAIN	GENOA AND FULL MAIN	GENOA AND FULL MAIN
4	11-16	MODERATE BREEZE	1	1.5	ONE REEF IN MAIN WORKING JIB	ONE REEF IN MAIN	GENOA AND FULL MAIN
5	17-21	FRESH BREEZE	2	2.5	TWO REEFS IN MAIN WORKING JIB	ONE REEF IN MAIN WORKING JIB	ONE REEF IN MAIN
6	22-27	STRONG BREEZE	3	4	THREE REEFS IN MAIN STORM JIB	TWO REEFS IN MAIN WORKING JIB	ONE REEF IN MAIN WORKING JIB
7	28-33	NEAR GALE	4	5.5	THREE REEFS IN MAIN MOTOR?	THREE REEFS IN MAIN STORM JIB	TWO REEFS IN MAIN WORKING JIB
8	34-40	GALE	5.5	7.5	THREE REEFS IN MAIN MOTOR?? VERY HEAVY GOING	THREE REEFS IN MAIN OR TRISAIL STORM JIB	THREE REEFS IN MAIN STORM JIB
9	41-47	SEVERE GALE	7	10	?	TRISAIL/STORM JIB/MOTOR VERY HEAVY GOING	TRISAIL STORM JIB
10	48-55	STORM	9	12.5		?	?
11	56-63	VIOLENT STORM	11	16			
12	64+	HURRICANE	14	?			

The table above is a yachtsman's Beaufort Scale. The wind and sea states are related to three typical modern yachts. One is a 20-foot cruising sloop with twin bilge keels. She is roomy, but not very powerful; she has an inboard diesel engine. The second is an able 32-foot cruiser-racer of moderate fin and skeg profile, built in the late 1960s or early 1970s. The last is a serious deep-water cruising yacht, designed and built to take rough weather in her stride. Each is assumed to have a three-slab reefing mainsail, a storm jib, a working jib and a genoa. They are all working to windward in open water. Below the heavy line each boat will experience considerable problems and eventually progress to windward becomes impossible.

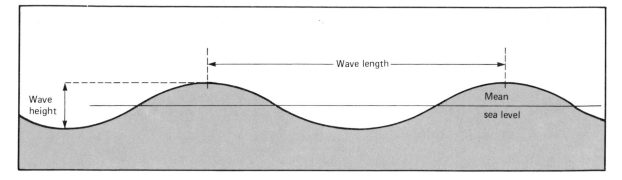

Waves

At sea in hard weather the three primary sources of danger are wind, sea state and poor visibility. Unless it rises to extremes, wind alone is rarely a problem for a well-found vessel. A good navigator, whether electronically assisted or not, can handle a lack of visibility effectively. Waves, however, are a different story.

Waves shake and wring a boat like a terrier with a rat, and sometimes they explode against her like a sledgehammer. They test her sternly every time she makes a passage and should she be found wanting in any of her many departments, we have problems.

Waves cause skipper and crew to get wet and in consequence cold. They make many of us seasick and can by this means reduce a capable hand to a human liability for the duration of a rough passage. Even if we are not sick, waves still make the yacht jump about like a carzy thing, rendering such niceties as cooking and navigation impossible sophistications.

Waves can also overwhelm us, roll us over and, in the end, drown us.

So we need to give them some serious thought. . .

Theoretical waves in deep, open water

When a breeze blows across mirror-calm water it causes the formation of perfectly shaped waves an even distance apart. At lower wind speeds these waves

Above: In theory, waves in deep, open water should assume a regular sine-wave profile. In practice the effects of wind and tide cause considerable variation.

approximate to the regular shape of a sine wave (see illustration). The distance between the wave crests is called the wave length and, if this is long enough, the waves will have a gentle enough gradient to cause no trouble to a small boat.

As wind velocities increase towards gale and storm force, wave shape tends to change, becoming steeper until finally the wave can no longer support itself and the strength of the wind blowing across the top helps it to break.

Wave height is measured from trough to crest (see diagram). If their development is unimpeded, the height of the waves caused by a steady wind in open water will go on increasing until they achieve the 'probable wave height' for that strength of wind (see the Beaufort Scale on page 10). Wave height depends upon *Fetch*, which is the distance that the wind has blown uninterrupted over open water. For example, the probable wave height developed in theory by a force 8 wind is given as 5.5 metres, but with a fetch of even 50 miles it is unlikely to exceed three metres.

Below: In a steady wind the height of the waves will increase as you travel further from the windward shore. This distance is known as the fetch.

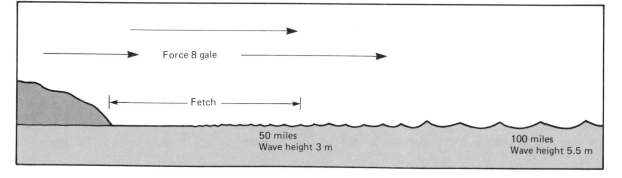

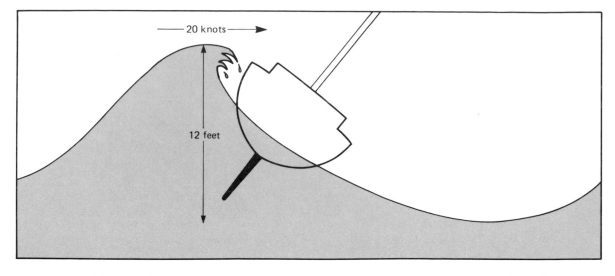

The *length of time* the wind has been blowing is also a factor in wave size. It takes many hours to build up to the theoretical mean wave height for a given wind force, so that in waters not open to the wide ocean it is unusual for these heights to be achieved during the average summer blow.

Wave speeds generally end up as about 60 per cent of the mean wind speed if it blows long enough for things to settle down to any degree of regularity.

The effect of all this is that a breaking wave in a moderate gale is likely to be 10 or 12 feet high, steep-sided and travelling at 20 knots or so. Not a pretty proposition, even though it is only the crest that is breaking.

Waves in practice

An ideal series of waves never normally appears at sea. This is because the wind varies, not only in strength, but also in direction. In any case, there is nearly always an old sea left over or another one coming from somewhere else, or both, or worse.

In real life, because of variations in wind velocity, all the waves in a given series do not travel at exactly the same speed, so from time to time one catches up with another. When this happens the two can combine to produce a wave half as big again as the regular wave height being experienced. These are *not* the 'freak waves' beloved of the media. They are predictable and appear in wave height tables as 'probable maximum wave height' (see Beaufort Scale on page 10).

Windshifts

The vast majority of gales and good solid blows will, at some stage of their lives, give their victims the benefit of a substantial windshift.

Above: Beam-on to a breaking wave in a gale...

I have waited eagerly for many a cold front to mark the beginning of the end of a gale in the North Atlantic, only to discover that as the scudding cloud breaks up and the wind veers to the north-west the sea gets a whole lot worse before it gets any better.

It stands to reason that if you have an established army of contented 20-foot seas marching uniformly out of the west and you suddenly remove their motive force to replace it with a new one from a different direction, the waves are going to get confused! Unfortunately, when they are subjected to this indignity they don't all suddenly execute a right wheel and stride away before the new wind. Instead, they maintain their progress towards the east while a new bunch begins marching over the top of them. The results are evil. Mostly the combatants sidle around one another, but when two big ones meet in confrontation they either rear up in a tower of breaking water and die noisily on the spot or they get together in a sort of lethal truce and go thundering away like a salt-water avalanche, very dangerously if you happen to be in the way.

The 'smooth'

Every so often the wave pattern (or lack of it) in a rough sea produces a short period when an area of water is relatively calm. These events are known as 'smooths'.

If you are going to carry out a manoeuvre such as tacking or gybing it is well worth waiting for a smooth. A smooth may be obvious or it may be merely a gap of a few seconds before the next big wave arrives. You may never get one, but if there is a smooth coming your way it is a lot easier to wait for it than to tack your ship in the face of a series of steep waves.

Tide and current

If you take a normal wave pattern and impose a weathergoing current upon it you will heap up the seas most wonderfully. The waves become shorter and steeper and break much more readily in consequence. In heavy conditions a bad sea may become dangerous as the tide turns to windward.

On the ocean you can often tell when you have run into an adverse current by observing the sea in even moderate weather. The tell-tale streaks of foam running down the backs of the waves as the current carries them to windward is the sign to look for.

In tidal waters the steepening effect on the waves as wind-with-tide changes through slack water to wind-against-tide is dramatic. Indeed, you can judge the turn of the tide on a windy day more accurately by observation than by referring to the tide tables.

Races and rips

In some places the nature of the seabed or the shape of a headland will cause the formation of *tide-induced waves*.

An uneven bottom can incite the running tide to upwell in whirlpools or stopper waves like a whitewater river.

Certain headlands and passages produce rough water, regardless of wind conditions. In the illustration the eddy running eastward along the south side of the headland meets the main stream in a mass of broken water that you enter at your peril.

These places are always far worse at spring tides than at neaps, and if you spice things up with an onshore gale of wind as well, you have a lethal combination. Sail into a bad tide-race on such a day and you may join the ghostly fleets of those who did not emerge to tell the tale.

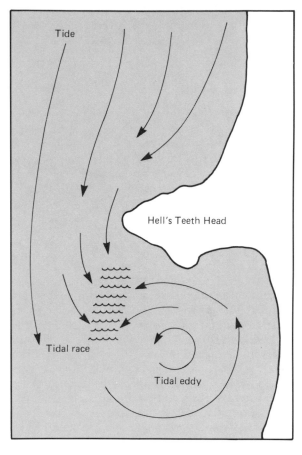

Above: An innocent-looking headland may conspire with the tide to create a race of blood-curdling ferocity. Such places are death-traps in heavy weather.
Below: A tidal stream upwelling over a rocky sea bed will often create a patch of angry, turbulent water.

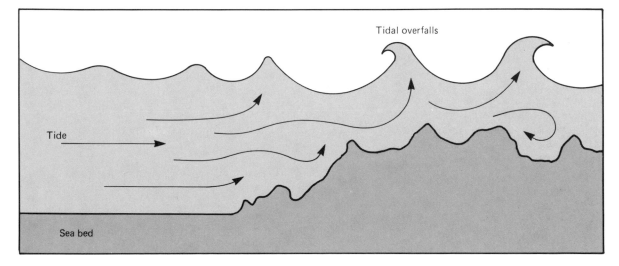

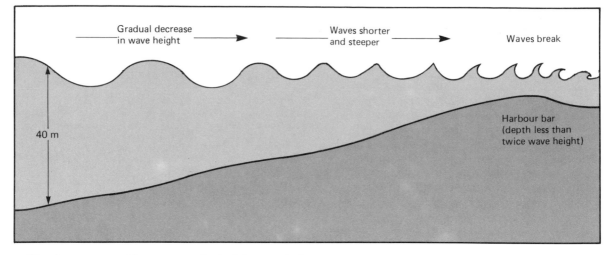

Above: In shoaling water the waves get shorter and steeper, and will often break over the harbour bar.

The dangers cannot be over-emphasied. I once tried to pass through the Race of St Albans in the English Channel soon after surviving two full-blown autumn storms in the North Atlantic. St Albans doesn't have a particularly ugly reputation, and it wasn't a bad day by comparison with my recent experiences, so I steered straight for it. As fortune dictated it was on top form. My boat was spun round and round. Steering was impossible. We gybed, came aback, square waves leapt aboard and filled the cockpit. Had we not seen what was coming in time and battened down we would have been swamped. To this day I have not seen a sea like it.

TREAT TIDE RACES WITH GREAT CARE!

Shallow water effects

Theoretical mean and maximum wave heights hold good only so long as the sea is deep enough to support them. Here is what happens when a series of waves enters shoaling water.

In a fresh to strong breeze the wave condition on a lee shore, even if fully formed, is unaffected until the water shoals to about 40 metres. From this point on the waves begin to ease a little, growing shorter and somewhat smaller. As the bottom comes closer the waves gradually become shorter still and take on a steeper shape. They are unwilling to break, however, until the depth has shoaled to between one and a half and two times the height of the wave, after which they cannot survive and break heavily.

If you are sailing anywhere near a lee shore in a blow you need to be aware of how the waves will react, particularly if you have to cross the bar of a river. Slip an ebbing tide under seas which are approaching their natural breaking point and you have another situation not to be tolerated. Countless well-found vessels have

completed their voyages only to be dumped terminally on the harbour bar at their destination – very likely by the first breaker of the falling tide. There has to be a first. Always bear in mind, if in doubt, that it may be waiting just for you. . .

Offlying banks are also subject to these effects. Sometimes they are marked as dangerous on the chart ('breaks in westerly gales', or 'breaks heavily'), but not always. If you are unsure, consult your pilot book but be ever wary in gale conditions, particularly if the tide is pouring into the eye of the wind.

Cliffs and breakwaters

When a sea runs squarely up to a wall it bounces straight back out again like a squash ball. It matters not whether the wall was put there by God or man!

In heavy weather the effects of this can be grim, so you should anticipate some severe nastiness if you are approaching a harbour with a wall that forms a lee shore with sea breaking against it.

Such a refuge would be a dubious option anyway, but waves bouncing back and running into one another add directly to each others' height and break with the ferocity of a tide-rip in full cry. A small vessel caught in a sea like this is liable to lose control of her destiny and she would be lucky indeed if the wind saw fit to squirt her in through the harbour entrance. The alternatives are to scrape clear with a bruised ego or be overwhelmed and wrecked.

The conditions such situations produce in a whole gale need to be experienced to be believed. Better by far to go elsewhere, or remain offshore where the big seas roll by more benevolently.

2. Fit for sea: the boat

The sea is no respecter of half measures. A boat and everything to do with her must be made as right as can be before she is taken offshore. In the halcyon days when proverbs were coined, the mariner was encouraged not to spoil his ship 'for a ha'p'orth of tar'. Put into the perspective of the late twentieth century it would be more realistic to consider the ruinous consequences of failing to replace a few hundred pounds worth of tired gear. There is no short cut. You just have to pay. Even if you do all your own work, you still have to buy materials, so it's 'groan you may, but go you must' when it comes to brassing up for your boat maintenance. There is no worse feeling for a seaman than looking aloft at a vital shackle he knows he should have replaced. Especially when his life may depend upon it.

You can get away with shoddy gear for months of sunshine yachting, but the first gale-force squall that catches you offshore will very likely reveal all.

A modern yacht can be divided into four main parts for the purposes of serious preparation for sea: the hull, the rig, the engine and the rest. We'll look at them one by one.

The hull

It goes without saying that so long as the hull is afloat the crew are in with a chance, so the watertight integrity of the hull must be the prime objective when listing your priorities.

In the case of all but the very lightest designs, fibreglass hulls stay pretty watertight so long as they do not run into anything. The same can be said of hulls built of ferrocement, steel and monocoque moulded wood. A traditional wooden hull is as good as its original construction and subsequent lifelong maintenance, and this may be at least as adequate as some of the others.

It is rare, in fact, for a hull to let itself down. More often it is the official holes in the hull which allow water in when they shouldn't.

Seacocks, including those for cockpit drains, must be regularly serviced, and their through-hull bolts checked for electrolysis.

Below: If the hull is watertight it will keep the crew above water when all seems lost.

Stern tubes should be in perfect order. It is sordid to sink because you lost your stuffing.

Hatches have got to be burst-proof. I have seen production forehatches I could kick my boot through, secured by catches that I would not put on a toilet door.

Companionway washboards need to have a lock-in facility, and the sliding hatch itself must be capable of being secured and opened from both above and below decks.

A substantial *bridge deck* or *companionway sill* should separate the cockpit from the main entrance to the accommodation.

Cockpit locker lids provide wonderful access for the sea if the boat is thrown over and they are not fastened down. A modern fat-sterned yacht has cavernous lockers which can take enough water to do a lot of harm.

When a boat is knocked down it is generally the windows on the leeward side which are damaged as the boat slams into the solid water in the trough of the wave. Contrary to what you might expect, this is like being dropped onto a concrete parking lot – so if your windows are not bullet proof they deserve storm boards when things are starting to look ugly. (If you have a wooden boat, you may prefer to keep some plywood and big nails handy and just nail the windows up if they break, but I can't say how the nails will hold in plastic. . .)

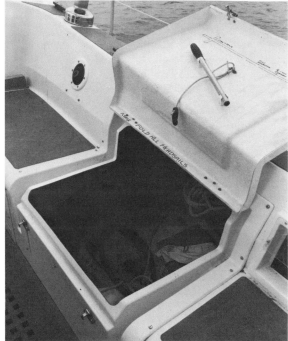

Above right: Make sure your forehatch is made of burst-proof material, and fitted with strong catches.
Right: If a locker lid falls open during a knockdown the sea will pour into the hole and could easily swamp the boat. Overhaul the catches regularly.
Below left and right: Companionway washboards must be solid, and capable of being locked and unlocked from outside (below) and inside (below right).

Once we start looking it's amazing how many extra apertures we pierce through our lovely watertight boats. To go to sea without complete confidence in the condition of all of them is just plain irresponsible.

Pumps

However good your arrangements for keeping the sea outboard, there is always a possibility of swamping, so every boat must have at least two effective pumps. One or more of these must be *manually operated* and one should work *from the engine*, either mechanically or electrically.

All pumps must display the following features:

● *Big capacity* 35 gallons per minute minimum, no matter how small the boat.

● *Big handle* It is no good having a wonderful hand pump if it has a cartoon handle exerting no more leverage than an eggspoon. The handle must have its own stowage near the pump for obvious reasons.

● *Comfortable siting* You need to be comfortable while pumping. Many production cruisers have a dinky handle stuck discreetly in a corner. If you can't go on pumping for fifteen minutes or more at a good rate, the device is a waste of time. Resite it, and if the handle is too short, buy a length of pipe and make up a proper one.

● *Readily clearable* Nearly all pumps can clog. It is vital that the guts are easily accessible. You may need to clear it in a hurry. Try it. Have you spare valves, diaphragms or impellors?

● *Good strum boxes* It can take as little as a match stalk to knock out a pump which stands alone between you and the Big Swim. A good filter or strum box at the suction end will go a long way towards making sure this doesn't happen, but remember that when the boat is flooded the water will pick up a load of extra debris from the lockers. Anything can choke a strum so be sure that every item with a high clogging capacity is well-stored.

● *A deep bilge* A flat-bottomed modern cruiser often has little or no bilge. In the event of taking on a quantity of water, not only will you have wet bunks but the pumps will not be able to suck unless the boat is put on an even keel, which may be inconvenient if you are engaged in a life and death beat off a lee shore (see page 55).

● *The engine pump* has the priceless advantage that it will work unattended, so if you are looking for a leak or sorting out a shambles on deck the bilge is still being cleared. Such a pump is also tireless, but *it must not be relied upon exclusively*.

The poor man's pump

When the world goes mad and all else has failed, it is amazing how much water can be moved with buckets.

Above: Check the siting of the bilge pump. Could you sit there and pump the boat dry? If not, resite it.

The more the merrier. There should be one for every crew member, plus one or two spares, then you can form a chain to bucket water out of the boat. If you have four people working efficiently you may be able to move up to fifty gallons per minute this way.

Remember that if you have a self-draining cockpit the water has only to go over the bridge deck into the cockpit to be drained overboard.

Rubber buckets with metal handles from building material suppliers are the best value. Don't buy the huge ones. They are too heavy to handle when full. They are also unwieldy and a problem to stow.

The rudder

Since time began, but particularly in recent years, rudders have been causing trouble. When you consider the forces to which they are subjected it's not surprising,

Above: A big spade rudder exerts a huge force on its pivot in a seaway.

Above: The bottom bearing of a skeg greatly strengthens the rudder.

Above: Supported throughout its length, this is the strongest of all.

The shearing strain on the shaft of a big spade rudder as it passes through its bottom bearing is enormous. It's hard to excuse fitting such an arrangement into a cruising yacht, but it's not difficult to understand why designers do it. These rudders are hydro-dynamically efficient and, being easily installed without all the expense of building a hull with a full keel or skeg they are cheap. Unfortunately they are also very vulnerable and many have failed. If you are stuck with such an unpleasantness, it is your duty to ensure that the shaft and its bearings are sufficiently overbuilt that they can never be a source of worry. It won't help to blame the designer who, after all, was only trying to keep the cost down, if you are left without steering in a storm on a lee shore.

It is safer to buy a boat with at least two beefy rudder bearings, one of which is at or near the bottom of the shaft, and then service them regularly.

Wheels

Too many steering systems fail in action, particularly on brand new boats. No properly balanced aft-cockpit yacht under 50 feet long should need a wheel, but if you have had one foisted upon you by fashion or because the boat is so ill-natured as to be uncontrollable without one, or even for so innocent a reason as the presence of a centre cockpit, you must check all cables, fittings, blocks, quadrants and the rest of the paraphernalia – particularly when it is new, for that is when most fail. Thereafter it must be done as often as seems necessary.

There must also be a readily accessible and properly functioning emergency tiller, which can be rapidly bolted to the top of the rudder stock if the wheel steering fails.

If you cannot be sure of your steering system, your boat should not put to sea.

Below: If you have wheel steering, make sure the end of the rudderstock will accept an emergency tiller.

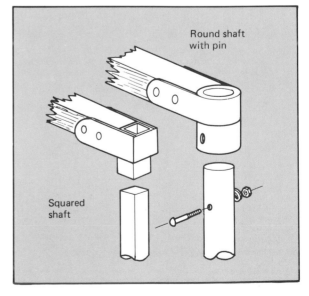

Round shaft with pin

Squared shaft

The rig

A yacht's rig needs to do two things. It has to be able to drive the boat through any state of wind and sea in which the hull is capable of being driven, and it mustn't fall over while doing so.

If the designer has done his job properly the rig should be able to deliver the basic requirements of propulsion. How well it delivers them and whether or not it fails in the process is up to you.

Sails and reefing

To be safe at sea in all weathers a boat must have a decent suit of sails in first class condition. The time a sail blows out will be the time you most need it, almost by definition. If you have a *roller reefing headsail* and you are hoping it will pull you to windward in a blow, it must be specially cut for the job. If this is so, it may work after a fashion when heavily reefed. If it isn't, by the time the sail

Below: A low-cut deck-scraping genoa can be an embarrassment in a heavy sea.

is rolled in to jib – or even storm jib – size it will set rather like a bin bag and be about as effective.

There is no doubt that a suit of purpose-built *headsails* including a couple of genoas, a small working jib and a bomb-proof storm jib, is a more seamanlike option. If your crew cannot cope with this, at least treat your boat to the best roller reefer you can buy. If you don't, she will never have the chance to sail herself out of real trouble.

A happy compromise adopted by some serious cutter owners is to set up the jib/genoa as a roller-reefer for convenience, but to have the staysail set on its inboard stay as a conventional and bomb-proof headsail, possibly with a reef in it. It can then be used on its own in really heavy going, balancing nicely with deep-reefed main or trisail (or mizzen if the boat is a ketch) and setting perfectly, no matter how hard it may blow.

The *mainsail* must be capable of being reefed down quickly to about half its luff length while still maintaining a good shape. If it is a roller-reefer and the boom droops after half-a-dozen rolls, a tapered batten attached to the boom thick end outboard will cure the problem. Nowadays, however, modern slab reefing is undoubtedly the best answer.

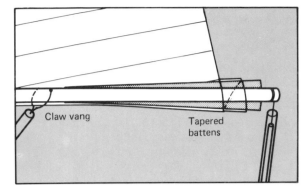

Above: Using tapered battens on a roller-reefed main.

A *trisail* is an important part of any yacht's sail wardrobe. In the case of some boats whose helm becomes dangerously unbalanced at the great angles of heel produced by sudden gusts, it is vital. I know of one popular 32-foot performance cruiser with a flattish bottom and 'fin and spade' configuration that sails along happily in force 7/8 with a trisail but whose manners deteriorate dreadfully under deep-reefed main. Trisails are good news because they don't use the boom, so if this should be disabled, all is not lost. They can be smaller than the deep-reefed main, providing another 'gear', and they are always 'fresh out of the bag'. They don't get much use, so they shouldn't blow out!

Below: The trisail sheets are led to winches via snatch blocks (left), the sail is fed into the track (middle) and the tack line made fast (right).

Above: When all is secure the trisail is hoisted on the main halyard. Note the two sheets passing each side of the boom.

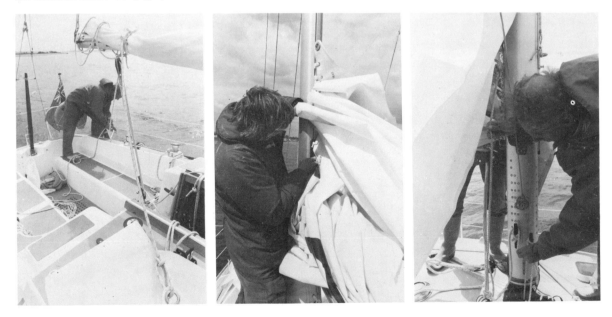

One final point: like a storm jib, there is no reason why a trisail should not be made from fluorescent orange cloth. White gets lost in the wave-tops in a gale and you might just as well increase your chances of being noticed as a bonus!

If your sails and gear are in order you have only to ensure that the rig stays in the boat. Spars, blocks, wire, rigging screws (turnbuckles), clevis pins, cotter pins, tee-terminals and all the rest are the easiest things on a boat to check, because you can see them. This is just as well, for failure of one is liable to lead to the loss of all and maybe yourself into the bargain .

Check round the deck systematically each day and whenever possible 'send a boy aloft' to do the same in harbour. When you are at sea, it is a good plan to check aloft each morning and evening with the ship's binoculars. You may spot a stranding wire just in time to save the day.

The engine

For any boat the engine, if fitted, is an important part of her ability to handle heavy weather.

There are three types of engine available to today's cruising yacht: inboard diesel or petrol (gasoline) and outboard.

Outboard engines can be discounted as being of any use to a yacht at sea. They are handy for scuttling around

Below: Outboard engines are of little value when the sea gets rough, and merely distract the helmsman from the business of steering the boat.

in flat water, but given even a moderate chop, the average outboard arrangement becomes worse than useless.

The only thing that needs to be said in connection with outboards and heavy weather is that the fuel tank must be firmly sealed, including its air vent screw. If you take a knockdown (an event more likely to occur in the smaller type of boat in which outboards tend to be fitted) you don't need fuel wandering around the boat to add to your problems.

An inboard engine, whether it is fuelled by diesel or – heaven forbid – petrol (gasoline) *must* start readily at all times, and it *must* keep running. There are no marine engines available nowadays which are fundamentally unreliable. If they become so it is only on account of slap-happy maintenance, or no maintenance at all.

Starting

If an engine cannot be hand started it is vital that it is equipped with a completely isolated *engine battery*. Without battery power there is no engine, so this must be available in profusion at all times. All terminals should be kept tight, spotlessly clean, and greased. The starter motor and alternator should be serviced at least once every two seasons and solenoid pump cut-offs (the device that stops a diesel with the starter key instead of a separate 'stop' button) should be regularly inspected. If this fails in the 'stop' mode, which can and does happen, you will probably flatten your batteries before you have sorted out what on earth is the matter.

Dirty fuel

Heavy weather will always search out any engine-stopping dirt that you have allowed to accumulate in your fuel system.

I once crossed the English Channel in a fine old vessel that had operated for years in the Solent with never a hiccup from her engine. Thirty miles out it died, strangled by the filth of ages stirred up from the bottom of the tanks by the rough sea. There were no spare filters, so we had no engine. Fortunately we did have plenty of searoom and a reasonable sailing performance, but different circumstances might have given us serious cause to regret our negligence.

Propellors

In a tumbling, turbulent sea there is no doubt that a slow-turning three-bladed propellor is far more useful than a two-bladed egg whisk, particularly one which folds. It is all very well having a 35 h.p. engine but that power must be transmitted to the water. A small propeller cavitating frantically just below and sometimes above the surface isn't going to succeed on a rough night.

The rest

Once you are confident that hull, rig and engine are truly seaworthy, all that remains is to ensure that everything moveable in the ship is in good order and is either permanently secured or capable of being properly stowed should the need arise. I was once advised by an old salt that so long as I prepared my boat for sea on the basis that she would at some time be flung on her beam ends, or further, I would not go far wrong.

That advice will always be sound and a vessel setting forth should hope for the best but prepare for the worst.

Securing down below

Most governing bodies of the sailing world now issue standards and suggestions for making sure a yacht is well-found in this respect. You could fare no better than to take such standards to heart, but all you really need to do is to go carefully through your boat and look at every item through the eyes of that supreme pessimist (or was he perhaps a realist?), my old salt.

You will find all heavy items of particular interest. A 12-volt battery, for example, landing on the inhabitant of the quarter berth, could extend his watch below into eternity. Low-flying ballast pigs make neat holes in the furniture, and good solid floor boards in free fall make a dreadful racket when they hit the deckhead. Unsecured locker lids turn a well-planned dinner into a premature lottery and should the stove take the opportunity for a walkabout it will probably spray the happy home with inflammable fuel as it enjoys a thoroughly smashing time.

No need to go on, is there?

Securing on deck

Working from the basis that all deck hamper such as boathooks, brooms, dinghies and the rest are normally well lashed down, there are one or two extra items requiring attention before the boat starts to jump about.

Water ingress is now of prime concern. Secure the *forehatch* (easily forgotten), and also any *windows* which may have been left 'cracked' for ventilation. Seal all *air vents* except proper 'dorade' boxes and check *cockpit lockers*. The *anchor chain pipe* is a source of water entry in many boats, so bung it up with a rag and a plastic bag if you've nothing better.

Any spare *anchors* should be below by this time and if you have one that is permanently stowed over the bow roller make sure it is solidly lashed, in the interests of both safety and quietness. No boat enjoys all that weight right out at the bow, but if you anchor frequently and sail always in sheltered waters, it makes sense to leave it thus stowed. Otherwise it should come inboard.

Flags don't last long if left flying in a gale so, for the sake of economy, lower them in good time. You'll also save some precious windage.

Spray dodgers are a source of great comfort in moderately windy weather but once the waves start breaking they should be stowed down below. I once took a heavy sea in a dodger lashed between two through-bolted lifeline stanchions. The stanchions carried away and so strong was the dodger that it took a couple of deckplanks with it! Never again.

Wherever your *Storm sails* are stowed they must be easily accessible and folded neatly, predictably and in such a manner that bending them on in a gale is at least possible. When trisail time comes along morale can easily be cracked by opening the bag and finding a big bunch of illegitimates instead of a willing ally.

Dealing with breakages

The strains imposed by heavy weather tend to multiply the chances of gear failure, and unlike the motorist, the yachtsman who 'breaks down' on passage cannot simply lift the nearest telephone and call his motoring

Below: A breakage like this could be terminal in a gale near a lee shore. Be prepared!

organisation to his assistance. The essence of seafaring is self-reliance and every boat which presumes to put to sea should be able to solve her own problems by using her own resources.

Tools

There is only one standard to apply to a toolkit for a boat venturing offshore: she must carry sufficient tools to enable a temporary repair to be effected on any part of her hull, machinery, or equipment.

Spares

Any vital item which cannot be fabricated on board and which is liable to fail should be backed up by a suitable spare. Unfortunately neither stowage space nor finance makes this an entirely practical proposition but there are many small items which can be carried conveniently which could well save the day.

Bolts and screws

Collecting a good 'fastenings box' is a lifetime's work. Having the right bolt 'in stock' should be a matter of pride for all skippers.

Rope 'string' and wire

A boat cannot carry too much cordage. Lots of small stuff in the 'string bag' will give you a choice of materials when you need to produce a lash-up. Sometimes wire is the only thing stable enough to lash two items together on a longterm basis. Galvanized fencing wire is cheap and can be obtained in suitable quantities from your local farmers' co-operative. This can also be used, stranded if necessary, as seizing wire to mouse shackles.

A plentiful supply of ducting tape is also a winner in a tight corner. It sticks to almost anything and is immensely strong once a few turns are on.

'Junk'

In addition to offical spares a boat needs all sorts of items for which, just at the moment, you can find no use. If you suffer a failure of major proportions, the most obscure piece of junk may be the one thing which, suitably modified, will get you going again.

How many lengths of timber, bent shackles, old inner tube, pieces of aluminium and mysterious rusty artefacts you ship is entirely a matter of character. Some of us are squirrels at heart, others abhor the inevitable mess somewhere in the boat, but whether you love rubbish or hate it, one day you'll need it.

Oh, and don't forget a couple of spare flashlights . . .

There is nothing about preparing a yacht for sea that a conscientious and observant person cannot achieve by the application of a little common sense. There are no mysteries and few clever tricks, just a realistic appraisal of how different everything is when the dock is far behind, the wind is piping up and you are on your own in the wild dark night. That is when you meet yourself and your work face to face, and thank the Lord you replaced that dodgy shackle.

An all-weather toolkit

The tools a boat will need before her skipper can say that she is equipped to deal with any emergency will depend upon her type, her size, the material of her hull, and many other variables. However, in addition to the obvious ones, there are a few extra items that many experienced sailors have found to be indispensable in an emergency. These are mostly of the sort which will exert large amounts of power where space and time may be at a premium. Here are some examples:

- An extra-large adjustable wrench
- A medium-sized pipe wrench (Stillson)
- A length of hollow steel pipe to slip over the end of any of the ship's heavier tools in order to achieve an irresistable leverage
- A one-handed sledge hammer
- A hefty cold chisel, kept good and sharp
- A number of hardwood wedges
- A steel wedge
- A dozen or so 6in, 8in, and 10in nails
- A small two-handed axe
- A set of bolt-croppers
- A wrecking bar

Many of these items will recommend themselves to imaginative seamen for sundry uses in addition to damage clearance...

3. The crew

'Ships are all right, it's the men in them. . . '

That remark was made in the long night before female suffrage. For our purposes, despite what my wife says, I think we can safely extend it to include both sexes and restate that no matter how well prepared our boats may be, they are only as good as their crews.

Crews vary enormously as to their resilience and ability. Often it is only when the going gets tough that you discover who you have taken aboard (even if they are members of the family) but whatever their strengths and weaknesses, all will respond to thoughtful treatment.

Food

There is nothing so important to a crew battling through a gale than regular, satisfying meals. Not only do they fortify the soul and fuel the body, they are also a natural mark of the passage of time, a social event, and about the only thing apart from your bunk that you've got to look forward to. It is a sign that morale is on the slide when the skipper says 'Don't bother about getting supper – it's every man for himself in the galley now.'

Routine is of tremendous importance and a good cook is a jewel beyond price. If there is no official cook and the rota is in danger of collapsing from intermittent seasickness, then it is time to call for volunteers. Volunteers, mark you not martyrs. The skipper will need to adjudicate and may well end up as 'doctor' himself for a while.

Cooking in rough weather is an art, but there are a few simple devices and techniques that will help a lot.

● A cook must be protected from the stove by a solid bar between him and his charge. Behind him, he needs a bum strap into which he can nestle coyly when he is rolled away from the task in hand.

● Wear bib-type oilskin bottoms. I know one beautiful woman whose legs still bear testimony to an unexpected knock-down.

● Use deep cooking vessels – don't mess around with that assassin, the frying pan. All pans must be clamped to

Right: A strong bar will protect the cook from the stove, and a strap will stop him falling backwards.

the stove with their handles turned inwards. Don't rely on the gimbals alone. They won't help you if sixteen-stone Sammy, the demon winch grinder, is hurled down the ladder and into the soup.

● In extremis, use only a pressure-cooker unpressurised but with the lid clamped on. If this leaps into the cook's lap, he may be able to field it before it scalds him to death.

● Whistling kettles with no lid are a good safe option.

● Keep meals simple and, if possible, easily washed up. Carry special hard weather rations, but if all else fails, there is always the 'five-day stew'. Every new addition brings fresh delights to the cockpit gourmets. Give it a new name each meal, perhaps to coincide with developing events. 'Casserole de la grande pooping', 'Soupe des plongeurs' or even the ultimate 'Bare pole bisque'.

● Serve hot drinks in *big* mugs, *half-full*. Not only do full mugs spill, but the contents blow in your face.

● Have a 'greedies' box full for the night watches. (Chocolate bars, pieces of cake, crocodile sandwiches – whatever they fancy).

● Help the victims to keep their meals down by giving preference to readily digested foods. Avoid rice salads with raw peppers and suchlike delicacies. They are just as colourful on their second viewing and their return by one will sap the morale of all.

Seasickness

This is probably the biggest problem facing any crew in bad weather. Very few people are completely immune, but the more fortunate only feel queasy and lazy. Heavy sufferers soon become convinced that only death can provide relief. These are likely to remain of no use to the ship until either the passage of time or arrival in port ends their misery.

With suitable encouragement some chronic sufferers are able to stand their watches and even enjoy themselves between bouts. Others throw in the towel and give up. For anyone, careful pacing helps tremendously.

If you are feeling sick, remember that the best position to adopt is flat out in your bunk, if necessary with a bucket alongside. You will feel much better. Resist the temptation to stay on deck whatever the odds because that is the road to exposure and complete moral breakdown. You may feel worse initially down below, but as soon as you are prone, things will improve. You may even drop into a doze which passes the time wonderfully. Then when you are needed, you will be ready and as fit as you are likely to be.

Try to eat if you can face it, otherwise don't. 'Sickbics' (dry, arrowroot biscuits) and water are a good start.

If you are the skipper you'll need to keep your navigating efforts to an efficient minimum because nothing churns the stomach like peering at a wet chart that's bouncing around (see Chapter 5). Watch your crew carefully for signs of seasickness: yawning, pallor, lack of interest and refusal to go below are all pointers to the approaching first vomit. Try giving a prospective sufferer an easy job, particularly steering. Often he will pull back from the brink, but if not even this saves the day, don't let him fall overboard as he throws up. People

Above: Don't let a seasickness victim follow her breakfast over the side...

being seasick lose all interest in everything else, including personal survival.

There are now a variety of medications available for motion sickness. In general there is no longer any need to rely on the ones which are guaranteed to make you drowsy. I have run a long-term experiment with many different crews using seasickness medications of the 'Stugeron' type and they proved to be effective for *most* people *when used as directed*. Don't reach for the medicine when you are already feeling ill. Read the instructions first!

Personal injury

Once she begins to jump about a small boat becomes an exceptionally dangerous environment. The possibilities for injury are many so one or more of her crew should be

---

Seasickness remedies

One hundred and fifty years before the first serious efforts were made to handle seasickness with medication, Charles Darwin wrote to his father, '...if it was not for seasickness, the whole world would be sailors'. This remark held good until immediately after World War II, when a chance discovery led to the development of the anti-histamine drug, Dramamine, as a cure for motion sickness. This, and other similar drugs, are generally taken orally and, for many people, undoubtedly ease the situation. Their main drawback is that they attack the symptom, which emanates from the balance control centre at the base of the brain, rather than the cause, which is disorientation of the body's main balance sensory

mechanism in the inner ear. In the doses required to prevent or cure seasickness these drugs tend to produce undesirable side-effects, such as drowsiness and a feeling of dryness in the mouth.

Late in the 1970s a new and more effective medication, Cinnarizine, became available. This worked directly on the cause of the problem in the inner ear. Like the anti-histamines this is also taken in tablet form and has been on the market for some time as 'Stugeron'. Its arrival has made such a difference to the offshore yachting scene that one wishes it could have been offered to the unhappy Mr Darwin, who wrote his letter home from the pit of despair after a week in the Bay of Biscay.

qualified to treat damaged personnel by having at least attended a first-aid course.

Most of the injuries sustained in small craft accidents are predictable and preventable. The skipper should be looking out all the time to make sure the crew do not make those mistakes which are likely to result in their being hurt. Here are some of the favourites:

● Burns and scalds in the galley: totally unnecessary if the precautions on page 24 are heeded.

● A sharp bang on the head from a flogging headsail clew or sheet. Don't let a sail flog with anyone near it; if it is unavoidable, warn the prospective victim to keep his or her head out of the way.

● Rope burns. These are usually caused by removing a round turn from a cleat or a winch so the sufferer is left holding a live, loaded rope. Don't let anyone commit such an atrocity.

● Crushed fingers or worse caused by playing fast and loose with ground tackle. Be on the watch for inexperienced crew unaware of the deadly danger. It's not difficult to lose a foot from being casual in this respect, and there are four-fingered sailormen everywhere.

● Broken or dislocated fingers where a rope has picked up on a wedding ring. Rings should be removed at sea as they have caused a number of such accidents.

● Wounds of all descriptions caused by rampant mainsheet travellers. If you gybe without making fast both sides of the traveller the car may whip across the track mincing everything in its path. If the car misses, the sheet itself is most effective at smashing spectacles on the face, or breaking expensive dentures. Secure both sides of the traveller at all times. And watch the boom!

● Broken bones caused by being thrown around, particularly down below. Fit plenty of solid grab handles where they are most needed.

● Falling down the companionway. Remind everyone to take their time. A broken pelvis from this accident is the nightmare of every singlehander.

● If you enjoy sailing barefoot you need to accept the odd broken toe with a straight face. Modern boats are veritable minefields of projections for the careless naturist. It's not only your toes that are vulnerable either. . .

● Never let the ship's engineer lean into the engine compartment wearing any loose clothing. An open shirt cuff may be caught by a whirling fanbelt, or a sportily hanging scarf could take a turn around the drive for the injector pump. The first may do no more than rip the garment from his back, but the effects of the second are depressing in the extreme.

● The injuries resulting from attempts to fend off one vessel from another (even a dinghy) or a vessel from a wall can be awful. The skipper must not allow anyone to try this. Even a three-ton yacht builds up far more

Below: Make sure your own harness fits properly.   *Below: Clip on before you come out of the companionway.*   *Below: To go forward, transfer the clip to the jackstay.*

momentum than a strong man can absorb in the space available. If the fenders are not to hand you'll have to grit your teeth and bear the crunch. Better to damage your capping rail than lose a limb.

● The dinghy. By far the greatest number of drownings among cruising yachtsmen occur between ship and shore. The dinghy is a dangerous place, particularly in a heavy blow. Now is the time to make sure all hands wear their lifejackets. It seems to me that a slavish rote of lifejacket wearing for good swimmers in stable dinghies in perfect conditions can lead only to contempt for a stupid rule. Save your authority until it matters, and then insist. (The other occasion to insist, even on a calm night, is when the crew come back from the pub. The booze has claimed even more victims than the gale when it comes to dinghy work.)

Safety harnesses

Without a doubt the most valuable pieces of safety gear on the ship are the safety harnesses. Every crew member should be issued with one at the outset of a passage and each should adjust it to fit correctly, with the 'pulling point' on the apex of the breast-bone.

All skippers will make their own rules about when harnesses should be used, but as a guideline, in really bad conditions I suggest you clip on before leaving the companionway and stay clipped on until you are back down below again. Certainly anyone leaving the cockpit for any reason – particularly to be sick – should be attached, and gents obeying the Call of Nature should be under orders to clip on. More than one body has been rolled up to the high water mark with its flies open. If things are desperate (the weather I mean) the cockpit drain is an invaluable aid to the incontinent.

Foul weather coats with integral harness attachments are a useful bonus because the biggest single reason why people don't bother with harnesses is the nuisance factor of clambering into them.

Boats should be equipped with life-lines (usually called jackstays) running along the deck so that you can remain clipped to the ship all the way from the cockpit to pulpit. Usually these are stainless steel wire, but a more friendly idea is to utilise nylon webbing which is immensely strong and has the advantage of being comparatively silent as a clip runs along it. Furthermore webbing doesn't roll beneath the boot and defeat its own object by throwing you over the guardrails.

Losing a man overboard is the worst thing that can happen short of actual shipwreck. Apart from commonsense and the survival instinct, the harness is the best assistance the skipper has for keeping the hands the right side of the wall. This is one part of a sailor's equipment where no money should be spared and where there should be no relaxing of the ship's stated rules.

Below: The clip slides down the jackstay as you move forward.

Below: Remember to follow the route of the jackstay.

Below: Make sure the line is long enough for the job.

Watch systems

It's as well to remember when deciding on a watch system that the ship comes first. The crew are there to serve the ship and if the ship arrives in safety at her destination then those of her crew who have not died of the plague, or fallen overboard, will do so too.

The crew can only serve their ship if they are alert and strong. In bad weather, sitting for four hours at a spray-swept helm fighting to keep the boat from broaching does not militate in favour of alertness and, after all that exertion, strength will be low on the list of the watchman's good points as well.

He or she needs sleep, leisure to eat meals and plenty of time below decks to ward off the incipient exposure or even hypothermia that lurk in the cockpit.

I have found that a system of shortened watches is a good idea in bad weather. Two hours out there are enough for anyone. Watches below are cut as well, but the blow won't go on for ever. You will be far more use to the ship after a rest – however short – than you would be at the beginning of your fourth hour on deck.

Each crew will work out a system to suit itself, but the guiding principle should be 'a short sharp watch on deck, followed by a well-spent watch below'. This gives the ship her best chance of being well served.

Sleep

To give an anxious part-time sailor unaccustomed to a bouncing, swishing 30-degree angle of heel any chance of sleep at all, a boat must be fitted with enough decent sea berths for the watch below. Solid leeboards are best because they give the greatest feeling of security, but a high leecloth is a good second.

As you look at the gleaming vessels on sale in any boat show, you will observe that such things are becoming optional extras in many production yachts. Maybe this is an indication from the manufacturers that they do not expect their products to go to sea. . .

If you are expecting to be offshore for only 24 hours or so, there is little harm in turning in 'all standing' if you don't feel up to getting undressed. It's better to lie on your bunk in your wet oilskins than make yourself sick looking for your stripey pyjama bottoms.

Below: A stout leeboard will keep the weary mariner in his bunk during his watch below.

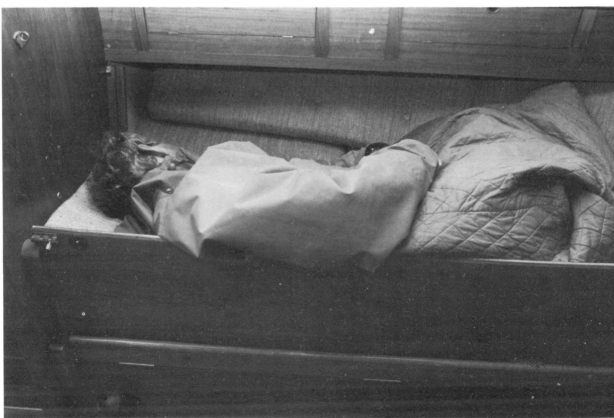

Clothes

If you read the glossy advertisements in the yachting press you will realise that it is now possible to kit yourself out with sailing gear which you will need a mortgage to pay for. It is obviously of paramount importance to keep warm and dry at sea but it pays to remember that until sportswear became big business people were climbing Everest in canvas anoraks and crossing the Atlantic wearing simple oilskins, souwesters and farming boots.

Don't get carried away. If you can afford the gear, buy it. It's great stuff. But don't spend money on multi-coloured 'team' oilies for all the crew when you are scratching around wondering whether or not to fork out the money for a trisail. If you wear any but the finest yachting boots, you'll have cold feet anyway.

Your basic heavy-weather kit should include simple, sound oilskins with high bottoms, a stout pair of light rubber boots, and *lots of real wool* (as worn by satisfied sheep the world over, and guaranteed to stay warm when wet).

Below: The author at the pump, in his heavy weather gear. Not quite the New York Yacht Club, perhaps...

The skipper

It is natural to feel anxiety when offshore in a small boat with the weather deteriorating seriously. The crew will feel that way and so will the skipper. The way he or she behaves can have a considerable effect on the emotional state of the rest of the crowd and hence upon the efficiency with which they serve the ship.

Skippers will approach this challenge from different angles depending on their own strengths and weaknesses, but some general suggestions may be helpful for those who, like most of us, are not natural leaders.

● Take all hands into your confidence. The crew need to feel they are a team and are acting together. If you share your decision-making process with them, explaining why you are adopting your chosen course, they will feel a great deal happier. If there are those on board whose opinion you consider of value, you may feel it is worthwhile to consult them. Whatever their advice, it will need to be handled with great tact.

What you must not do is appear indecisive for this is an admission that you feel the anxiety which everyone else is trying to suppress. By all means share your doubts. If it helps you to resolve them quickly, but do not try to mitigate your own anxieties by loading them onto others who are looking to you for strength.

● Delegate as much of the work as possible while doing your share, and then show faith in those to whom you have delegated. This will not only give you the chance to save yourself until you may be needed, but it will involve more crew members in the responsible running of the ship, which assists the vital feeling of teamwork.

● Encourage weaker crew members to 'do their bit' of the watchkeeping. Even someone almost too sick to care can be detailed off to look out to leeward from the shelter of the best spot in the cockpit. If he doesn't feel he is helping he begins to harbour a black mood of failure and despair. His morale sinks to the bottom of the sea and his gloomy presence upsets the rest of the hands. He will also be sheepish when it's over and you all stride ashore to boast to one another of your deeds. And that's a shame.

● The ability of an outfit to deal with hard weather begins with a wellfound vessel, but in the end it depends on the crew giving the ship the chance to do herself justice. When you are considering options, your correct assessment of their ability could be of vital importance. It doesn't do to ask too much from a weak group if you have the choice of another course of action, but if the same group is faced with no choice at all, then how they come through will depend to a great extent on the amount of thought you put into leading them. A little deliberation is worth a lot of brute strength.

4. Handling the boat

Each point of sailing brings its own challenge, but in heavy weather it is the ability to work to windward and keep on doing so without breaking up that is the final arbiter between one boat and another. Sail shape is of vital importance to this ability, and whether a skipper is getting it right or not should be a question asked by every marine insurance company.

Headsails

At low wind speeds the greater the curvature of a sail, the greater is its power. If you sheet your jib in too tight on a gentle day the boat dies under you. Ease the sheet, and she points just as well and comes back to life. By doing this you have put the right shape into the sail to enable it to do its job. Its maximum camber (the 'high point' of its curve) will be about 40 per cent of the way from luff to leech.

If you have a 'stretch luff' sail the halyard tension will have a direct effect upon this curvature. Use the halyard winch to set up the camber of your sail until it is right for that wind speed; then adjust the sheet.

As the wind stiffens you will find that the camber moves aft and the sail becomes baggy. When this happens the sail is 'dragging' more and 'lifting' less. It is making the boat heel excessively, and it is slowing her down. To get the sail back to scratch you should wind up the halyard, watching the sail carefully, until the camber is back where you want it. If your sails don't have this facility your only option is to harden the sheet still further.

When the wind is so strong that these adjustments will no longer pull a close-hauled headsail into shape it is time to change down and begin the process again.

The smaller sail will be cut a little flatter because it is designed for stronger winds. Were it cut full it would continue to drag the boat over and down to leeward.

For hard winds then, you are looking for a sail of the correct area to produce the necessary power, with just the right degree of camber and *no more*.

If you have a *roller reefing headsail* you will find an effective sail shape increasingly difficult to achieve as the wind pipes up. Such a sail is usually cut to perform best when fully unrolled in a true wind of force 3–4. It is

Below: If the halyard is slack (left) the maximum camber in the sail will be well aft (centre). Tension the halyard to move the camber forward (right).

unlikely that the aft portion which is left setting after you have rolled in the first third of the camber will come anywhere near producing the sort of lift you need. You may also be suffering a great deal of headstay sag, giving your headsail a curved luff at a time when it is crying out for a straight one. In addition, as you roll sail around the headfoil, you create a lump of dead windage which the air has to climb around before it gets a bite on the sail itself. However, the device will save you from getting wet feet once in a while. Are you sure you want one?

For those whose boat is too big for them to sail properly otherwise, it does seem that the cutter with a conventional staysail inside the roller genoa has much to recommend it.

The mainsail

The same premises apply to mainsail shape as to headsails. At each stage of reefing, the degree and position of camber are vital.

With a modern mainsail there are plenty of controls to achieve this. Halyard, outhaul, traveller and vang (kicking strap) are minimum equipment on most cruisers nowadays. The illustrations make it clear what to do with the halyard and the outhaul to shape up the mainsail. The vang (kicking strap) is more interesting.

The function of the vang is to control leech tension. Ease it off and the boom rises, allowing the upper part of

Above: Even the best roller genoas work at a disadvantage when the first third of the camber is rolled onto the headstay.

Below: A slack main halyard (left) gives a baggy sail. More tension (right) pulls the camber forward and improves efficiency, particularly at the top.

Below: A loose outhaul (left) increases camber in the bottom third of the mainsail. Tightening the outhaul (right) reduces the camber for strong winds.

the leech to twist away. This twist is an important factor in how well the sail works. If there is too much twist the sail will spill wind from the upper portion, but if there is too little the upper third of the sail may stall and simply drag the boat sideways, making her heel as it does so. A good rule of thumb for twist is to use the vang to line up the top batten of the sail with the boom. This should ensure maximum lift and minimum drag. In practice the mainsheet and vang work together to maintain leech tension when you are close-hauled. As you move further away from the wind and want to ease the sheet the vang will keep up the good work.

Once you have *shaped* the mainsail using halyard, outhaul, vang and sheet, you need to *set it* at the correct angle to the airflow. This is where the traveller comes in. In heavy weather you will have been working to get the sail nice and flat, but if you set the traveller in the centre and ease the sheet to trim the sail, the twist will go to pieces and the sail will become fuller into the bargain.

To prevent this, ease the traveller down to leeward instead of letting off the sheet. Watch the sail carefully for 'breaking' at the luff. If the boat is driving well with a good headsail and the helm feels balanced, it's not important if the sail lifts a little; however, let it lift too much and you are back to excess drag once more. Put another reef in, mate. It's about time.

Below: If the vang is loose (left) the boom rises and the top of the sail twists away. Tighten the vang to keep the twist under control (right).

Shortening sail

It is all very well to chat glibly about 'changing down' and 'putting in another reef'. The mechanics of switching headsails are obvious enough but how to set about the job in a bad blow and not either drown or at least soak the foredeck hands is something else entirely.

Thought is the answer. Somehow you need to turn that leaping sprayswept foredeck into a haven of peace for long enough for your least favourite crew member to go up there and do the business.

The one thing you don't do is simply send him forward while the boat is crashing along. Here are three suggestions that will cover most circumstances:

1 Steer 'shy'

Ease main and headsail sheets to something like a close-reaching position and then steer a touch 'above' close-hauled. this way you can, by using the helm, slow the boat down to as near a controlled standstill as the seas will allow. You probably won't choose to let the speed fall much below three knots for fear of losing your grip, but the foredeck hand will really appreciate your trouble.

Incidentally, in all these drops *don't let go the sheet* before the sail is on the deck. Unless you have a racing headfoil, you'll find you can still drag the beast down by

Below: Use the mainsheet to shape the sail, and the traveller to set it. Here the mainsheet is kept constant as the traveller is dropped to leeward.

the luff on most boats and avoiding a flogging sail will be well worth the energy consumed.

2 Run off

The surest way to put any headsail to sleep is to blanket it behind the main. Steer as near as you dare go to a dead run, easing off the mainsheet as you bear away. Sheet in the jib or genoa fairly tightly so that the foot is inside the guardrail and then send your crew forward. The sail will come down like a lamb, the sheet can be released and the change made. It is *most important* to keep the sail sheeted home until it hits the deck because otherwise it

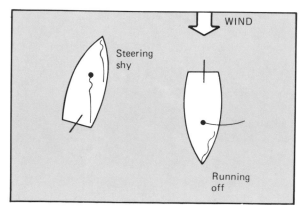

Above: Two ways of damping down the headsail – steering shy to take the power out of it, and running off the blanket it behind the main.

may 'gybe' itself as the hands are working and knock them over the wall.

3 Heave-to

When you don't want to give away an inch of ground to windward, but no-one is interested in going on the foredeck until the boat is stopped, then heave-to. Put the helm down as if to come about, but instead of letting go the jib sheet, keep it made fast so that the sail falls aback on the new tack. Once the boat is through the wind she will rapidly lose way and you should then put the helm down to leeward again. You are now hove-to. A heavy displacement boat will stop if you do this. A modern flat-bottomed yacht with a short keel and a spade rudder will not behave herself nearly as well but she will still give the foredeck brigade an easier ride than the rodeo-style alternative.

When the boat is stable in the hove-to state you have simply to let off the headsail halyard (*not* the sheet) and drag the sail down. Obviously, as the sail comes off, the boat's hove-to equilibrium will be upset, but she won't go far without a jib so this will not matter.

One advantage of this method is that when you heave-to you may be able to lash the helm down and walk away. The helmsman is thus freed from his post to go and do his share of the work up forward.

Below: To heave-to, put the helm down (left) with the jibsheets cleated. The jib backs (centre), and once through the wind the boat settles down (right).

Above: Reefing the mainsail – first dump the vang.

Above: Set up the topping lift to slacken the leech.
Below: Ease the main halyard and pull down some sail.

Reefing the mainsail

Here again, the skipper's thoughts in bad weather should always be moving in the direction of how best to achieve the result he needs with a minimum of morale-sapping discomfort.

Steering shy is good in a modern boat that will remain under control when the mainsheet is let off. Heaving-to is good in any boat; in a short-handed heavy gaff cutter with a long boom it is the only safe way.

The technique of reefing

Reefing is a similar process in every fore-and-aft rigged boat I have ever sailed except those fitted with roller gear. The only notable difference is that on a modern cruiser with a five-man crew it can be done in under 20 seconds, while on my own 30-ton gaffer it takes my wife, my mate and myself about a quarter of an hour. Because it's so easy in a modern yacht such vessels can always show the breeze the right amount of sail and a husband and wife team should be capable of doing the job in not much more than one minute. If it takes you upwards of two then something is wrong, either with your gear or your practice. Here's how it goes:

1. Dump the vang (kicking strap).
2. Set up the topping lift.
3. Ease the main halyard and hook on the new reef tack cringle.
4. Set up the main halyard to hold the tack on.
5. Dump the mainsheet and pull down the new clew cringle using the ready-rove reef pennant (winch, tackle or manpower, the principle's the same).

Below: Hook on the new tack cringle (left) and set up the main halyard to hold it on (right).

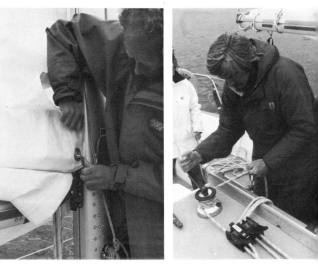

6. Secure the pennant, ease away the topping lift, and immediately set up the sheet and vang so as to flog the sail for as short a time as possible.

7. Tidy up. This may mean tying in the reef points, though on a short-boomed masthead sloop this is rarely necessary except in the worst weather. Take such a liberty with a big mainsail, however, and I won't come to your funeral.

Helming to windward

In rough seas any but the heaviest, most powerful boat needs sympathetic steering. The danger is that you build up speed and then literally fly off the crest of a wave to land with a nerve-shattering crash in the trough with no chance of building up speed again before the next wave stops you altogether.

It is a happy coincidence that the boats most prone to this wretched habit are the ones best able to mitigate its effects. The modern, race-influenced flat-bottomed cruiser is a demon for the pounding, but she is also extremely quick on the helm, giving the driver every opportunity to avoid the problem if he is sufficiently skilful and not tired out by the process.

The heavy displacement pre-war yacht or working vessel will be far too slow on the tiller to do much to help herself, but these boats generally have the momentum to drive on through, albeit somewhat wetly. They are, however, easy to steer in a seaway. Hit the groove and keep them there and they will do the rest. If the wave length is such that a boat of this type doesn't like it, all you can do is bear away ten degrees and try again.

Above: This yacht is under good control running under deep-reefed mainsail only.

Below: Pull down the new clew cringle using the reef pennant. Secure it and ease the topping lift.

Below: On many boats it is not always necessary to tie in the reef points along the boom.

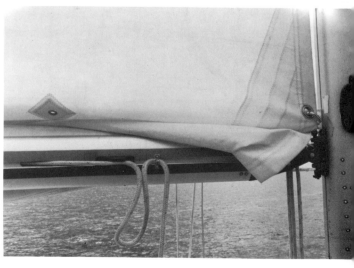

The rig powers up enormously for every ten degrees further off the wind you go between 40 and 70 degrees. By the time such a vessel has settled for 55 or 60 degrees she should be unstoppable.

The technique in the lighter, quicker boats is as follows: Keep an eye on each wave as it approaches, then luff the boat gently towards the crest, bearing away sharply as you get there and sailing further off the wind down its back. Repeat the process for each wave and you will average out at a useful angle to the true wind and give your crew a tolerable ride.

The problem is that a high degree of skill is required to do this effectively, and considerable endurance is needed to continue doing so for an extended period. It is not insignificant that top offshore racing boats now carry specialist 'upwind helmsman'.

Whatever you are sailing, the message is to keep her moving. High pointing will mean slow speed in heavy weather. Slow speed means excessive leeway and that is not to be tolerated.

Motorsailing

It is inherent in the physics of the matter that when she is closehauled a boat is developing less forward drive from a given apparent wind than on any other point of sailing. In calm water this rarely presents any difficulties to a good sailing boat, but when the tremendous stopping power of a head sea is inserted into the equation, the windward performance of all but the finest yachts can deteriorate alarmingly.

When you are being stopped in this way, the application of a little power can make all the difference. The boat will point higher, leeway will be cut down, she will never miss her tacks and she will drive ahead in an altogether more satisfactory manner.

Unless she has a really big engine, a sailing boat generally doesn't do well motoring straight into a sea, but cracked off to 30 or 40 degrees with a well-reefed mainsail set she will manage better, even if you choose not to use a headsail at all.

Reaching

When reaching in a steep sea the danger is that you will be thrown down by a wave that takes you beam on. Since you are heeled to leeward anyway, it won't have far to knock you and because of this you can never carry as much sail in rough water as you would in calm, even though you need it desperately to drive you through the jumble.

The best solution is to turn towards any evil-looking waves and then bear away down the back once more, as when sailing to windward. Any boat can do this when

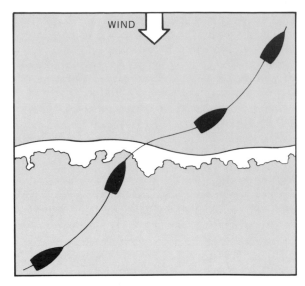

Above: Considerable skill is needed to steer a light boat to windward in a rough sea by luffing towards the crest of each wave and bearing away down the back.

reaching, and all types can benefit from it. It probably won't be necessary to luff head to wind. Altering course sufficiently to take the wave on the shoulder rather than on the beam should do the trick. You'll have to duck to dodge the spray though.

If the wind is well abaft the beam and you are not concerned about getting to leeward of your course an interesting alternative is to bear away, catch the wave and go surfing. This is great fun – until you broach and get rolled over. Treat surfing with respect. It has its place but you need the services of an alert, natural helmsman to be halfway sure of your security.

Running

When running at sea in hard weather the greatest danger is that of being *broached* by a big wave. If you slew round to windward the extra momentum of your turn will increase your chances of a bad knockdown, while if you perform the dreaded leeward broach you will enjoy all this plus the bonus of an all-standing gybe.

In order to avoid these possibilities you should first make sure that you have the corrtect amount of sail up. Too little and you won't have proper control; too much and you will run up to your maximum hull speed and develop serious steering difficulties. Most boats steer contentedly at the sort of speed they could make to windward in calm water, which is something like the square root of their waterline sailing length – about five knots for a 28-footer.

The next thing to be sure of is that the mainsail, if set, has a meaty preventer rigged from the boom end to the bow of the boat. The ideal arrangement is to lead this through a snatch block on the foredeck and then bring it aft to a spare winch, so you can slip it from the safety of the cockpit in an emergency.

Headsails, if the main is set, should be boomed out firmly to windward.

The important thing with both sails is that the clews should be held *rigid*. If they can swing about they will increase the boat's natural tendency to roll.

When only one sail is required, some boats are quite happy to run under a deep-reefed main. Others would be difficult to steer like this and behave better with a lone headsail or 'front wheel drive' arrangement.

Steering through a roll is an art which any dinghy helmsman will have developed, but the big-boat sailor may need advice on how best to do it.

As the boat rolls to leeward she will need a lot of weather helm to hold her straight. As she comes upright and rolls up to windward, lee helm will be called for quickly to stop her careering off by the lee and gybing.

This is because the centre of effort of the rig is moving from outboard on one side of the yacht to outboard on the other, and on each side it exerts a force which, if unopposed, pulls her off course. The effect is aggravated by the natural tendency of a heeled vessel to turn towards the side on which her keel is extended.

In a dinghy, it's quite simple: get it wrong and you are swimming. In most weather the cruiser will let you off lightly but in a real gale your mistake could have results that will remind you of your dinghy days. . .

Below: When the boat rolls the distance between the centre of effort (CE) and centre of lateral resistance (CLR) increases, and she tries to broach.

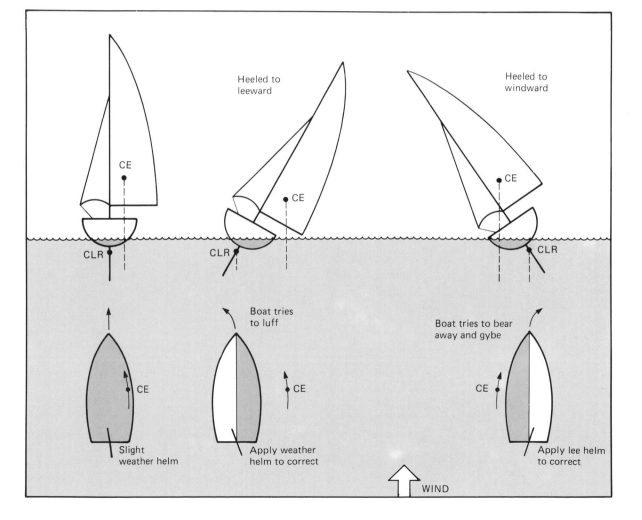

The golden rules when running are:
- Get your speed and choice of sail right.
- Keep your sails rigidly under control.
- Steer with great care.
- Never forget about the 'apparent wind factor'. This is the point of sailing where your judgement of wind speed is most vulnerable.

Below: When running before a gale, rig a preventer to stop the mainsail gybing accidentally.

Squalls

It is all too easy in an increasingly mechanised world to rely on a forecast and ignore the evidence of our own eyes. Squalls are mini-storms that move across the water. They may be self-contained or they may be part of a larger weather system, but it is always easy to see them coming in fair weather or foul.

Squally weather occurs frequently along the cold front of a temperate depression, but squalls abound in tropical seas as well.

Generally a squall takes the form of a heavy cloud. As a rule of thumb, if you can see the horizon underneath it then it will not be too severe. But if it has a full 'skirt' that is blotting out the horizon you are in for a soaking at the very least, and maybe a heavy wind as well.

Avoiding a squall

If all other considerations are equal it is always worth dodging a squall if you can. You can 'plot' its approach just as you would a ship at sea, and establish whether or not it is on a collision course. If both edges of the squall are changing their bearings in the same direction it is going to miss you. If one edge is opening one way and the other the opposite, then it is spreading its arms in welcome. Try a course alteration and see if it makes any difference. If it does you may be able to duck it successfully.

Assessing a squall

We have already seen that the 'skirted' squall guarantees its victims a soaking. The big question is, will it produce wind or not? The answer is that at a distance you simply cannot tell by looking at it. I once suffered a series of four apparently identical squalls one afternoon in the Caribbean. The first three brought only delicious cooling rain, and the fourth blew out my mainsail!

If there are boats between you and the squall watch them carefully. Are they falling over or sailing on unaffected?

When the squall is much closer you will be able to see if the wind is cutting up the water – but by then it may be too late. Be ready to go into one of your squall tactics.

Once the squall is upon you, you can place some reliance on the ancient saw:

When the rain's before the wind, tops'l sheets and halyards mind.
When the wind's before the rain, top'sl soon you'll set again.

In other words, if the rain hits you before the wind does, watch out!

Line squalls

Line squalls can be found in any latitude although certain locations favour their formation. They are particularly popular, for example, in the Inter Tropical Convergence Zone, and also on the east coast of North America, where their movements are often forecast with a high degree of accuracy on the continuous weather bulletins broadcast on VHF.

They can be recognized by a long line of cloud advancing athwart the wind direction. Sometimes the cloud appears to be rolling over upon itself and frequently an arch-like phenomenon will be seen at the centre. You can sometimes see the horizon under the cloud of a line squall, but in spite of this, it may produce winds of alarming ferocity.

Beware of line squalls.

Squall tactics

If you suffer a sudden blow that you know will not last, there are three simple tactics for handling it without drama.

Shorten sail Depending on your boat and your crew strength you may feel this is too much trouble, but it is very easy just to drop your headsail on deck and put a few ties around it. It is even easier to roll it up if you have the gear. This simple reduction will be more than adequate to ride through most squalls.

Heave-to Particularly if the wind is forward of the beam, heaving-to provides an easy way of reducing the strains produced by a passing squall. This is, of course, no use if you are sailing with a genoa as the spreaders may damage it as it lies aback. The boat will not balance properly either.

Run off If you are laid over by a squall when reaching, the best solution is to run off square before the wind. This will not only reduce the apparent wind, it will also have the effect of bringing the boat upright once more. Do not think that because you are running with the wind you are necessarily increasing the time that you will be under the squall. The wind may not be blowing in the direction of the squall's advance, and even if it is, your boat speed will not make a great deal of difference to the situation.

It is unusual for a squall to affect one boat for more than about 15 minutes, but those 15 minutes will be very different from the shambles they could have been if the boat is well handled.

Below: This squall has blotted out part of the horizon.

5. Navigation

Navigation can be defined as the art and science of directing the course of a vessel from one point to another in safety and in the shortest reasonable time.

On a clear sunny day the process presents no problems, but when the weather takes a turn for the worse the job can, if you allow it, become increasingly difficult. By the time conditions are really heavy, chartwork and the question of the boat's whereabouts may have degenerated into a nightmare lottery.

There aren't a lot of laughs attached to being navigator in a gale, but before we look at some of the ways in which you can pace yourself and continue to produce the desired result, let's identify the enemy.

Seasickness can turn every trip to the chart table into a gruelling and messy test of character. It can also tempt you to do less than even the minimum of essential work.

The *motion* of the boat and the general degree of *wetness* everywhere make meticulous chartwork almost impossible.

Often heavy weather aggravates your misery by serving up some *thick visibility* to put the cap on your joy.

Even if visibility is not too bad, spotting buoys as both they and you ride up and down on different 15-foot waves is far from easy. It also becomes difficult to count the time sequences of lights.

Estimating leeway is almost impossible as your boat is hurled around by the seas, but you can be sure it is greater than you think.

Distance logs can become erratic as a light hull leaps from wave-top to wave-top. Many an impellor ends up measuring enough air speed to render the record of 'distance run' a nonsense. Your best bet is an old-fashioned heavy trailing log with a long line. The windage on the short line of a lightweight trailing log has been known to flip the whole thing out of the sea!

The *course steered* is unlikely to be very close to the course you ordered up and the damping of even the best

Below: As the weather gets worse your navigational accuracy will deteriorate too. You should convert all your course lines to 'cones' and take care to keep them well clear of dangers such as lee shores.

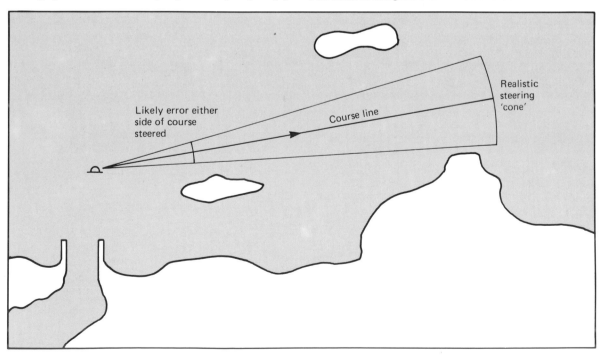

Likely error either side of course steered

Course line

Realistic steering 'cone'

handbearing compasses is not enough to ensure a clear bearing in a very rough sea.

You must also beware of the effect of, for example, thunderstorms if you are relying on an *electronic fixing device* such as a Decca or Loran 'C'. The advice of certain manufacturers that you should rely on their products' integral DR computer working from the last good fix while thunderstorms are in the vicinity should be treated with the contempt it deserves.

All these delights, together with others too numerous to mention, do not militate in favour of nit-picking chartwork. Instead you need to make a realistic assessment of the degree of accuracy you can hope to work to and plan your course accordingly. Don't on any account neglect to allow for your deteriorated personal performance or you may demand of yourself more than you have to give, and end up by submitting to seasickness and exhaustion.

The lines which you draw, both physically and metaphorically, between danger and safety must be a lot further from the edge of disaster than you might choose on a calm day. Because every part of your operation is less accurate you need to allow a greater margin for not being where you hope you might be. Instead of a course line being the width of a pencil point, you should at least consider that it may have become a tight cone spreading out from your point of departure. The angle of the root of the cone is the likely helming error. If the cone brushes too close to a danger, then you should adjust the course required accordingly. If that sets the cone into danger on the other side, then you'll have to keep a particularly sharp lookout, go somewhere else, or fire the helmsman.

When you are working up an *Estimated Position* (EP) the same thing will apply, but you should bear in mind that the gale may also be affecting the tide strength and direction. Your tide vector will become less positive and instead of an EP you will have an *estimated area of position*. As always, assume you are in the corner of the area nearest to danger, before deciding where to go next.

Position fixing is often a shaky procedure in heavy weather. Use transits wherever possible as a source of position lines. They are always accurate, quick to observe and easy to plot.

Compass bearings may be wildly inaccurate and you should spare yourself those sick-making sessions squinting through a compass prism by using the ship herself and the steering compass whenever possible. If your mark is nearly ahead, or astern, steer directly for it (or away from it) for a few seconds and read the ship's heading. This is a particularly useful method of checking whether or not you are the right side of a clearing line if you are skirting an area of danger.

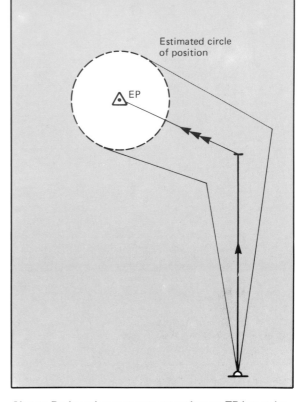

Above: Reduced accuracy means that an EP has to be inflated into an estimated area of position.
Below: Using the boat as a bearing compass.

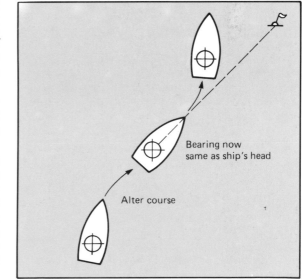

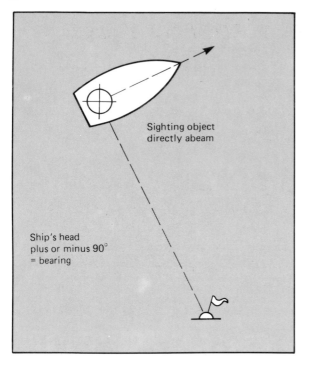

Above: Taking a bearing on an object directly abeam using the ship's compass.

You can get a good bearing on an object by sighting it directly abeam down the mainsheet traveller, or anything else that runs athwartships. Add or subtract 90 degrees from the ship's heading and you have its rough bearing.

Organisation

If you know the weather is going to get rough, do as much work as you can before the boat starts leaping about. You can calculate in good time any tidal heights for port entry, stream vectors, critical bearings and offlying dangers and any amount of other details while you still feel like the King of the Castle. If you leave such work till you feel sick and tired of the whole business it is only too easy to either not bother at all or to make a stupid and dangerous mistake.

Rough weather is the time that *tidiness* at the chart table really pays dividends. Have more than one chart out at a time and they will surely jump the fiddle into the puddle under the companionway. You won't have time in your brief visits to the 'office' to search for pencils and plotters. They *must* be where they *always* are. I keep my pencil in the working page of the log book; the book is then closed – and impervious to drips – and the pencil is always where I want it. Dividers can pin the cook to his galley very effectively if the boat throws them properly, so don't give them the chance. Drill a hole in one corner of the chart table and keep your dividers plugged into it.

Electronic navigation aids which have a facility that tells you whether you are on track, or off it to the right or left, and how far, can be a Godsend when even moving from the helm is an effort of will. However, the apparent excellence of this information may lead to fatal mistakes if it is not checked from time to time with information from another source – such as your own eyes. The very fact that these machines are rarely far wrong lulls the unwary into a highly dangerous sense of security. YOU MUST KEEP A PLOT AS WELL, because that is the only check you have on a small box which you did not personally assemble and to which you may well be entrusting your life and the lives of your crew. If it should prove to be in error, and you have delegated to it your whole responsibility, then a place on the statistics list is deservedly yours.

At all times keep your navigation as *simple as possible*. If you don't think you need to fix your position, don't try to do so just because it happens to be exactly an hour since you last did so. If you can tell where you are well enough simply by looking, be happy to settle for that. Stay healthy, stay where the action is, or rest yourself for when you will be needed.

But don't allow lethargy to fool you into doing too little. Think clearly, even if it takes a positive effort to get your brain into top gear. Once the current item of navigation is dealt with you can always go and have a snooze at the helm which, for some of us, beats agonising in the bunk. A session at the chart table can sap your strength as surely as a trip to the foredeck, so ration your visits and *make each one pay*.

6 Strategy, tactics and the weather

Unless you are the sort of person who goes out looking for trouble, avoidance of heavy weather has to be better than involvement. This can mean being on the opposite side of the world to miss a hurricane season or simply making a temporary course alteration to steer round the worst of a squall.

If you are not in a position to keep clear of the blow, then acting sensibly upon a shrewd assessment of developments will help to ease the unpleasantness.

You should be using all the available data to try and stay one step ahead of the weather. Nowadays the information you need can be drawn from many sources. The natural ones have been used since Noah looked skywards on the Fortieth Day, while man-made ones are increasing in number every year. Some are expensive, others are free, but none are worth the candle unless the information they supply is interpreted with wisdom and acted upon positively.

Long-term strategy

Strategy for a sailor is the art of being in the right place at the right time.

Anyone with a choice in the matter would never think of crossing the North Atlantic in winter. If he did so and he made it in one piece he would survive only as proof of the Everlasting Mercy. All published opinion on the subject advises strongly against rounding the Horn between April and November while any sailor sufficiently deaf to the experience of ages to attempt a trade wind crossing from Europe to the Caribbean in August will have only himself to blame for a slow passage, a bloody nose, or maybe even a one-way ticket to Davy Jones' Locker.

The official Pilot Books for all the oceans give the general tendencies for wind and wave as the seasons change. *World Cruising Routes, Ocean Passages for the World*, 'Routing charts', and, of course, accounts by sailors who have been there before can all be considered.

Strategy won't guarantee you an easy ride. If you have to cross any ocean north or south of 35 degrees you may be served up a gale to sharpen your wits even in high summer, but if you stick within the limits imposed by a mature appraisal of world weather patterns, you are giving yourself the best chance of not meeting something you can't handle.

The weather forecast

Weather forecasting may be official and professional or you may do it yourself by observing barometer, sky, wind, precipitation, wave pattern, visibility, temperature and whether or not your rheumatism is playing up. Both types of prediction are of great importance.

Radio forecasts

These are by far the most important sources of overall weather information for yachtsmen.

In Britain the BBC do a wonderful job by broadcasting a synopsis and forecast four times a day. You can receive Long Wave Radio 4 from the Azores to the Arctic Circle so within those limits there is no excuse for anyone who understands English not to be informed. In the United States the meteorological channels on VHF broadcast continuously, giving the synopsis and local forecasts for the adjacent coastal waters.

Sea areas are big places, however, and local conditions can be expected to vary from the general forecast. Most countries issue excellent inshore waters forecasts by radio to cope with this. Times and frequencies of these are published in the Nautical Almanacs but if you don't speak the local language you may find the information less than helpful unless you are well prepared.

To understand a foreign shipping forecast, you need to be able to count from one to ten in the language concerned, and you need to be able to recognise a few vital words. Choose a yachtsman's pilot book for your cruise area which contains a good glossary. Never mind a translation of 'cucumber', what about 'south-west gale'?

If you have studied the form of the foreign forecast and are aware of the boundaries of the sea areas to which it refers, its message will be clear enough.

While you are within range of coast radio stations it is always worth keeping your VHF radio switched on in heavy weather. It will keep you abreast of any navigational warnings, and in the UK important weather information is given out as soon as it is issued by the Meteorological Office. Gale warnings are repeated,

Above: Your first sign of an approaching blow is likely to be a gale warning. This may not be for you, but for sea areas between you and an approaching weather system. By using the synopsis to predict what is likely to happen, and checking this against the reports of coast radio stations, you may get up to 24 hours' notice of a gale coming your way.

Above: A sky like this, a falling barometer and a backing and strengthening wind add up to bad news. Add a heavy swell coming with the wind and things are starting to look interesting. If the barometer is falling at a rate of 6mb or more in three hours then hang on to your hat, for this is a guarantee of winds approaching gale force.

new gale warnings are reported and, if you have missed a BBC forecast, the salient features will be given out again in due course.

All this, however, is somewhat pedestrian when compared with developments such as Navtex and Weatherfax machines. If you have enough money and you enjoy being well-informed, all you need do is push the button (sometimes you don't have to make even that much effort) and all the information that is currently available showers down onto your chart table. These machines will become cheaper and cheaper as years go by until they become as affordable as echo-sounders. But we still shan't be off the hook. An echo sounder in the hands of a novice does no more than tell him how deep the water is at a particular time and place. To an expert it can provide the key to a whole world of knowledge.

However excellent your data and predictions from the outside world may be, what counts in the end is what is happening to your ship *right now*, and what you deduce is going to happen in the hours to come.

Ocean forecasting

Unless you have all the necessary communications technology, once out on the wide ocean you're on your own. You may be lucky enough to speak to a ship who will pass you a weather report but mostly you are left with your own observations. Fortunately, while mid-

ocean gales are often stronger than those experienced around land masses they are rarely as dangerous because there is nothing for you to run into out there. Your chances of foundering in deep water are far less than your chances of a terminal encounter with the rocks, cliffs, tide-rips and lee shores of coastal waters.

Tactics

If your strategy has failed, and you run into the heavy weather you were hoping to escape, your first priority is to avoid running into anything more solid than the wind or the waves.

The danger to be averted at all costs is that of letting yourself be placed in a perilous position from which your boat does not have the sail and/or engine power to extricate herself. Usually this means being directly to windward and far too close to a chunk of land or an offlying shoal. Any location where there is too little water to float your boat and onto which the wind is blowing is called a *lee shore* and must be avoided in heavy weather like the ship-eater that it is.

The options

You have two basic options: you can go *for shelter*, to windward or to leeward; or you can *stay at sea* and either carry on regardless or win sea room and ride it out.

Going for shelter

Once you have decided to act on the assumption that conditions will soon become hard to tolerate you need to make one big decision: 'Can I, or can I not, reach suitable shelter before this blow is upon me?'

If conditions are intolerable already the question is not a lot different. 'Can I safely arrive at and enter a suitable haven during this blow?'

To answer either of these you will have to consult the chart and see what harbours or anchorages are available.

Running to leeward You will find it much easier to reach shelter which lies to leeward than to windward; the question is, will it be safe to enter when you get there? You may be lucky and find an anchorage like Millpond Bay in the illustration, which would be a good option in this wind. It is more likely, however, that a coastline to leeward will look like Snug Harbour, which you would be unwise to approach unless you could be certain of arriving before the onset of the gale.

Below: If you decide to go for shelter, check out the options carefullly. An all-weather haven like Snug Harbour may be ideal, but will you reach it in time?

If your chosen shelter lies some distance off it is wise to bear in mind any major windshifts which may be upon you before you get there. Is there a front due, for instance? If so, will the shifting wind make the harbour untenable, or its entrance unusable?

Take a bad gamble on these quesions and you could be in for some disappointing results, but whatever your decision, if dirty weather is in the offing follow the advice of Lord Nelson, and 'Lose not a moment'. If you reef too soon when driving for shelter, you could rob yourself of the extra knot of speed you needed to reach safety before the first 60-knot squall. Give the boat her head; in the end it may pay handsomely.

Working to windward Look at the coastline in the illustration with the wind blowing offshore instead of on. Snug Harbour is now an all-weather haven. Take the opportunity and get in while you can. Once inside you will still be safe even if the wind shifts 180 degrees. Entry under those conditions would be suicide, but that's not your problem any more.

If you are confident the wind will stay put, even Deadman's Bight has become a good spot to be.

If you are caught well offshore in deteriorating conditions there is a great deal to be said for trying to

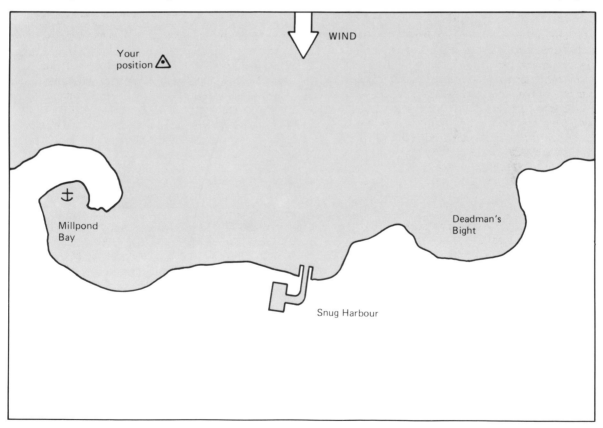

reach shelter in the nearest safe harbour to windward. The closer you get, the easier the sea will become. This will increase your chances in a rising gale, and if things turn out so badly that you don't make it, and end up hove-to, you will have earned yourself a few extra miles of searoom.

Staying at sea

Carrying on regardless When your destination is distant, and especially if it lies to leeward and you have plenty of searoom, it is not unlikely that you will decide to carry on. You may well feel that whatever this blow may send, it isn't going to affect your progress in any way other than to make you wet, cold and miserable. Just make sure that you have taken all the precautions discussed in Chapter 2 to make your boat watertight and ready for a bouncing.

Switch to your heavy weather watch routine. Bend on your storm canvas in good time. Stoke up the five-day stew, make sure the baby is sympathetically stowed, and keep on yachting.

Increasing searoom If the strength of the gale is such, or likely to become such, that carrying on is out of the question for your boat, and if there is no reachable shelter to windward and no safe shelter to leeward, you have no choice left but to ride it out at sea.

Above: Think before you run for a harbour mouth in a heavy breeze. It may look like this when you get there! If there are no other options you would be well advised to ride out the gale at sea.

This is never a popular decision. No-one enjoys 24 hours of being stood on his or her head under an icy firehose of abrasive seawater. But if you make it clear to the hands that the alternative may well be even less savoury, they usually back you up in the end. Swimming in 25-foot breakers holds little appeal, even for the most seasick sailors.

The tactics you may choose to adopt for riding out the gale are discussed in Chapter 9, but whatever you decide to do you will require all the searoom you can get. If there is a choice, work out which shore is going to be the dangerous one and then use all available means to place yourself as far away from it as conditions will allow.

Once you are confident that you are far enough off you can jog to windward, heave-to or even lie a'hull (see Chapter 9) if you have to, but until you have plenty of searoom you can never afford to relax.

Remember, it is nearly always the shore, an offlying danger or a tide rip that brings a vessel to her final paying off. Only rarely does the sea manage it unaided.

7 Shelter from the storm

When all else has failed and your boat is driving down onto a lee shore despite all your efforts with the sails and engine, you still have your ground tackle. Anchoring off the beach has been known to save vessels that could have otherwise been lost. There is no special secret for this; the same principles apply as in any other circumstances:

● Use the biggest and best anchor you can carry.
● Use the longest possible scope of cable.

We all have our own favourite type of anchor. You'd hate mine, so I won't try to force it on you. Just buy a really good one, and *make it big*. Don't expect the toy that arrives as part of a production boat package to be good for more than a lunch hook.

Cable is a more complicated subject. *Chain cable* has much in its favour. By virtue of its weight it assists the holding power of an anchor. For the same reason it requires a shorter scope than rope, or to put it another way, a given scope will do more good! Chain doesn't chafe, either on the stem head or the sea bed, so it won't part in the night. It is easy to clean and it self-stows if you have a decent chain locker.

Below: A length of nylon warp shackled to the anchor chain will give elasticity to your heavy tackle.

On the other hand it is noisy, expensive and if it is heavy enough to do any good, it will require the services of a windlass in any boat much over 32 feet long. A windlass should be a meaty piece of equipment with a proper handle sited so that a person can throw his weight at it. *Not* a toy-town, useless piece of aluminium, discreetly placed in the chain locker almost out of reach below the foredeck.

The hidden problem of chain cable is that in exceptionally violent conditions, no matter what the scope, it can still snub up bar tight. If this happens you are in danger of plucking out your anchor, and this is where nylon warp comes in.

Nylon warp is super-springy. Its elasticity gives it tremendous strength and a boat riding to it will never snatch at her anchor. It is cheaper than chain and can be used on larger boats without a windlass, but it is subject to chafe. Furthermore, to give an anchor with warp the holding power it would have with chain you will need twice as much scope.

The best solution for heavy weather anchoring, particularly on a lee shore in a bad sea, is to ease out a long scope of chain and then shackle a hefty length of nylon warp into the bight of the chain before it has all run out. This gives the best of both worlds. If your anchor won't hold now, you can do no more.

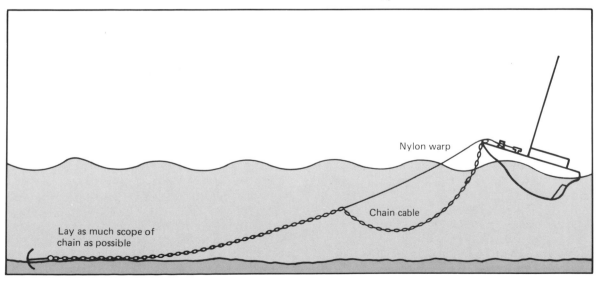

Nylon warp

Chain cable

Lay as much scope of chain as possible

Selecting a berth

Once you have arrived at your chosen anchorage you have to decide where to lie. You'll be looking for a spot as close as possible to a weather shore, keeping the fetch down to a minimum but taking account of any predicted windshifts. You don't want to swing up the beach in the night and since you are going to lay a monumental scope of cable, swinging room is something to be taken seriously.

Given that you have plenty of good tackle and your boat behaves herself at anchor (see Chapter 8) your greatest danger is that of other boats dragging down on you. Foresee it, and select a berth that will minimise this possibility.

Lying to two anchors

If you are lying in a sheltered roadstead with no particular tide affecting you it will do no harm to lay a second anchor if you are in doubt about whether your bower (main anchor) will hold.

The best way to arrange the anchors is a Y-shape from the bows. If your bower is on chain and your kedge is on warp and chain (even if the cable is all rope there should be *at least* two fathoms of chain between the end of the warp and the anchor) you can pull in on the kedge warp until you see the bower cable sag a little. This shows that the weight is coming off it. The anchors are then balanced, with each taking some of the load.

Below: If you need to lie to two anchors lay them in Y-formation, adjusting them as you swing.

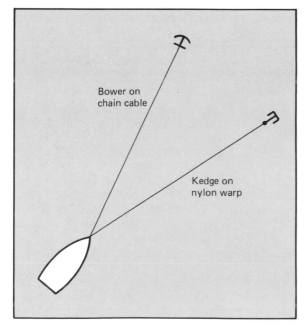

Bower on
chain cable

Kedge on
nylon warp

Laying a second anchor

If your bower is on chain and you have a decent dinghy, the best way to lay your kedge is simply to row it out. Make sure your foot is not trapped in the coil when you heave it over the stern! If both your anchors are on warp you can generally motor up to where you want to place your kedge, gathering slack on the bower warp as you do so. You can then drop the kedge and fall back, evening up the warps as you go. If you have a handy boat it is quite possible to sail up to the spot for letting go the kedge, but personally I'd use the excuse to give the batteries a good charge.

Swinging with two anchors down

If you should swing more than a few degrees when you are lying to two anchors, you will need to adjust the cables to even up the pull. If you swing so far that they come into line they may well interfere with one another so that you have to recover one and relay it. A thorough nuisance. It is much less trouble to lie to one reliable anchor and lots of scope.

Weighting the cable

An excellent way of augmenting the holding power of an anchor without increasing the scope of the cable is to lower a weight down the cable so that it is suspended halfway to the sea bed. This has the effect of holding the cable down so that it pulls on the anchor at a more efficient angle. It also resists the tendency to snub. Patent weights designed for this purpose are available, but you can always make one up by shackling a spare anchor, a pig of ballast, or a suitably loaded mutineer into the bight of the cable and lowering away.

Windage

The windage of your boat's hull, mast and superstructure is something over which you have no control, but there is plenty of additional windage that you can do something to reduce. If it is going to be touch and go for your anchor, every little helps.

Here are some of the items which are easily removed and which could make all the difference:
● Dodgers and sprayhoods can add up to a sail area equivalent to a sizeable trisail!
● Flags, burgees and washing.
● Stowed sails, particularly furled roller headsails.
● Radar reflectors.
● External halyards (take them down and leave a light 'sleeper' up there, but only if you are staying put.
● Any other deck hamper.
● And finally, don't forget that the sail area of three fat men standing scratching themselves on the foredeck is substantial.

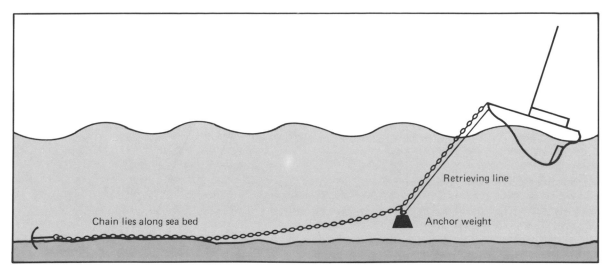

Above: A big anchor weight lowered down the cable on a big shackle holds the chain at an efficient angle to the sea bed and reduces the risk of snubbing. It will also stop the boat surging around and let you sleep.

Moorings

If there are vacant mooring buoys in your harbour of refuge it is always tempting to use one instead of anchoring. If you are considering doing this, there are one or two rules to apply.

Never lie to a mooring unless you have good reason to believe that it is in first class condition, and of a suitable size for your boat.

Never lie for more than a few minutes to a slip rope as these are prone to chafe. In rough weather it is best to shackle your anchor chain to the mooring if you can stand the noise, because doing so will remove any danger resulting from chafe. This is a rather cumbersome procedure, however, and if there is a chance of wanting to leave in a hurry it may be best to avoid it.

It is a sound idea to lie to a round turn and a bowline. The round turn will absorb the chafe and if you make the bowline good and long you will be able to untie it without going into an attitude of prayer over the bow.

If you are going to make fast with a line or with your chain, leave a slip rope on the buoy as a back-up. The slip rope also serves to relieve the main mooring line while you are tying or untying it.

Top right: Having picked up the mooring using a slip rope, double up with a second warp tied with a round turn and a bowline. Leave the slip rope in place.
Right: If necessary, shackle your anchor chain to the mooring in place of the warp.

Lying alongside

Raft-ups are always a mixed blessing. If the boats are arranged in a sensible order of size and are properly tied up, then so long as no-one wants to leave and the water remains calm you may get some sleep. Should the situation be deficient in any of these requirements bad tempers and broken boats are the inevitable result. Raft-ups are particularly to be avoided in heavy weather. If the water chops up you can guarantee that someone's fenders will jump up over the rail and then there will be trouble.

Probably the most dangerous contingency is that of two boats rolling together and damaging one another's spreaders. This can be avoided by making sure that no two masts are adjacent.

To lie on the inside of a raft in a berth that is rapidly becoming untenable while those outside you vacillate is a wretched position to be in. The way to be sure of never experiencing it is to have nothing to do with raft ups-on windy days. It may be tempting to go for the imaginary security of the dock wall and the crowd, but you could well be much safer, and you will certainly be a lot quieter, if you anchor away from the mob.

The weather berth

When you are being blown hard against a wall to which you have tied yourself you must make sure you are not pinned onto it by the rising wind and sea. You must also make certain you don't suffer damage while struggling to get off.

Above: Beware of tying up to a lee shore.

When you need to leave an ugly weather berth there are a number of ways to help the boat off the wall. The first thing to try is bearing off with a spar. You'll probably use a boathook or spinnaker pole. If it's blowing hard this may not work but you may find you are able to spring off by either the head or the stern.

Below: By careful manipulation of warps, fenders and engine power it may be possible to spring the boat off a weather berth.

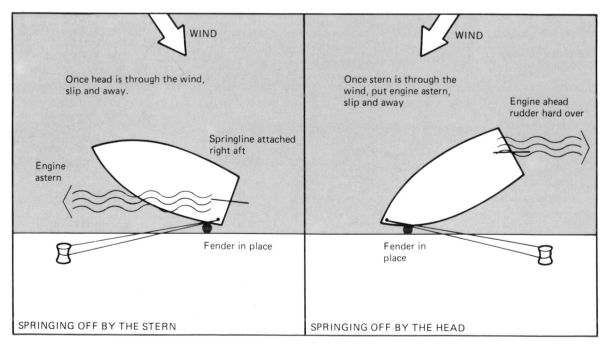

WIND

Once head is through the wind, slip and away.

Engine astern

Springline attached right aft

Fender in place

SPRINGING OFF BY THE STERN

WIND

Once stern is through the wind, put engine astern, slip and away

Engine ahead rudder hard over

Fender in place

SPRINGING OFF BY THE HEAD

This should do the trick, but if not you will need to pull yourself off. If there is a handy post, mooring buoy or some other fixed object up to windward row a line over, bring it back to the foredeck and pull – or winch – the ship's head up to the wind. If you've no foredeck windlass, you can rig a snatch block near the bow and lead the line to a sheet winch.

If there is nothing to secure a line to you will have to kedge off. Row your kedge well out to windward and then proceed as above.

When circumstances are such that your boat is pounding in a weather berth and there is no available alternative you can ease the pain by rowing out your kedge amidships and using it to hold yourself off the wall.

Fenders

These are obviously the secret to survival on a hostile wall. Like anchors, fenders need to be BIG. Take the manufacturer's recommendation, double it and you are on the way to success, but far more effective in extreme cases is the humble honest *motor tyre*. These can be acquired from most dumps at the popular price and conversion to the world's most effective boat-saver consists of gouging two holes in the tread, one at the top for the rope and one at the bottom to let the dirty water

drain out. If you have white topsides the resulting black marks may be unacceptable so you should prepare three of these fenders before you need them by stitching them into canvas covers. If you haven't time, hang some canvas down the topsides 'inside' the tyres.

Motor tyres are also better than plastic fenders if you are drying out beside a wall, while without their canvas and hung over your seaward side, they present the maximum deterrent to any smart yachts approaching with intent to raft.

Clearing out

Any roadstead or harbour with one side open to the sea has the capacity to change from a sheltered haven into a deadly trap at the caprice of the weather.

As soon as the wind begins to blast straight into your anchorage it's time to go. Never mind what the others are doing. If in doubt, clear out; particularly if night is coming on and you know you would be safer at sea. It doesn't happen often, but when it does you'll know what you have to do. With luck there will be another bay around the corner, open to the previous wind direction but now sheltered, to which you can shift your berth. If there isn't, you will just have to grab as much searoom as you can and then ride it out. Many a boat has been saved by doing so.

Below: If there is a suitable post or mooring ring to windward you may be able to warp the boat off the wall using the anchor windlass or a sheet winch.

Below: If all else fails, hold the boat off the wall using the kedge, attaching the stern line to the kedge line with a rolling hitch.

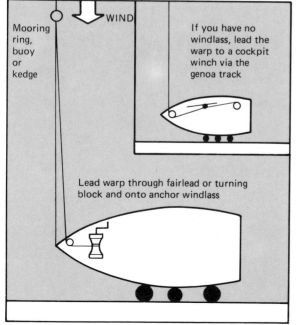

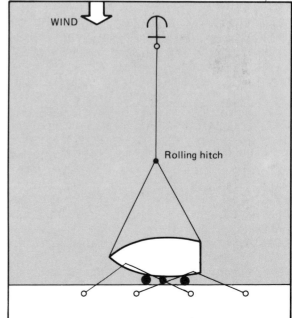

8. Boat Performance

When we are talking about the 'performance' of a motor car we tend to think in terms of its acceleration, top speed and roadholding. It isn't quite like that with sailing boats. There are aspects of their performance, irrelevant on a normal yachting day, which become immensely important in difficult conditions.

To say that any yacht must be a compromise is one of the clichés of the sport but it is nonetheless perfectly true. The problem lies in deciding not whether, but what, you are prepared to compromise. An edge of performance in wind strengths under force 3 perhaps, or your personal safety in an open-sea gale? A certain amount of volume, or the ability to heave-to? Five degrees of pointing to windward in calm water, or the capacity to go straight with a lashed helm for long enough to let you have a comfortable brew?

Boats vary so much that before it is possible to discuss how you can set about surviving a bad blow it is necessary to look at some of their different characteristics, and the way these may affect your options.

Three types for comparison

Sailing boat design has developed down so many different avenues that it is impossible to deal with them all in this book. The question of multihull seaworthiness, for example, excites so much controversy in comparison with the number of multihulls afloat that I propose to steer clear of it altogther.

The other most sizeable group that is not represented here is that of twin bilge keel yachts, but if you own one of these useful cruising boats you should be able to draw your own conclusions from the information that follows. The types to be studied are:

Boat A A long-keeled, heavy displacement cruiser.
Boat B A moderate fin and skeg profile cruiser-racer of the late 1960s.
Boat C A light, beamy, flat-bottomed fin and spade fast cruiser of the 1980s showing clearly the influence of the current International Offshore Rule (IOR).

Because this is a book about heavy weather sailing we are only going to look at features of the boats which directly affect their hard weather performance. The relevance may be slight or even reversed when cruising around in good, or moderately poor conditions. Since most of us spend the majority of our sailing lives successfully avoiding a reckoning with the Great Examiner, the designers of many modern production boats are able to ignore some serious shortcomings in the ultimate ability of their products.

In case that sounds like a mere statement of opinion, let's examine some of the general elements that help a boat deal effectively with dreadful weather and be specific about how well endowed with these qualities each of our three yachts may be.

Working to windward

Boat A Probably not so close-winded as the other two owing to her less dynamically efficient keel shape and the fact that her rig may well be of a lower aspect ratio. These will not stop her getting to windward, but she will need to be sailed freer than the others. She should be a powerful sail carrier but she is going to give her crew a wet ride.

Boat B A great windward performer in a blow. Close-winded, powerful and quick enough on the helm to steer over each wave if you need to. Faster to windward than boat A, and even wetter in consequence.

Boat C Because she is light, this boats needs less canvas than the others to drive her, which is a useful feature. Rig and keel are highly efficient, so she points and foots well, but she needs careful steering. A moment's inattention and she slams into the trough, waking the sleepers even if they are feigning death, and effectively stopping her. On account of her high degree of buoyancy and large freeboard she should be the driest of the three.

Directional stability

A boat that dances and yaws perpetually about her course is tiring for her helmsman who will consequently be more apt to make a serious mistake when running. Even if he manages to make no errors, his morale will be sapped and he will become exhausted earlier than he otherwise would.

Boat A A joy to steer. A long keel and plenty of draught well aft keep her moving straight and true. If she rolls or heels her easy sections will cause no serious change in helm balance.

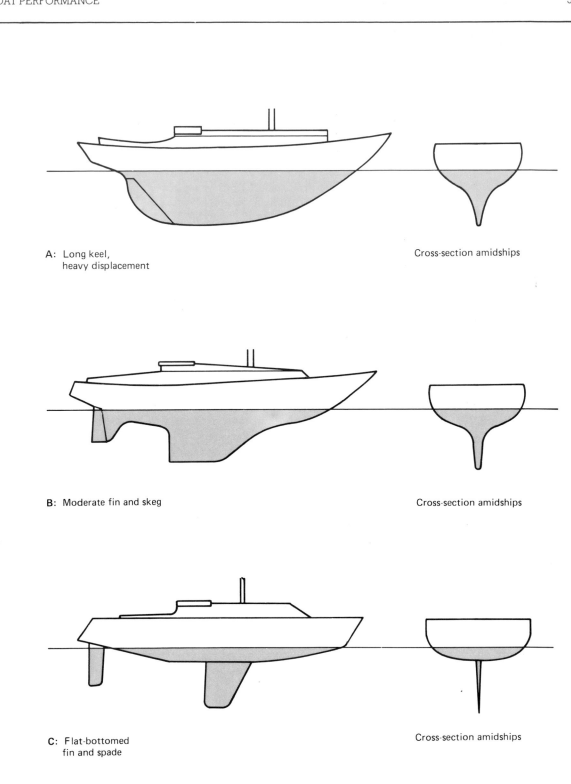

A: Long keel,
   heavy displacement

Cross-section amidships

B: Moderate fin and skeg

Cross-section amidships

C: Flat-bottomed
   fin and spade

Cross-section amidships

Boat B   Much quicker on the helm than boat A. She will be simple enough to steer with the wind forward of the beam, but as it moves aft she may become rather a trial. Her sections are sufficiently natural to enable her to maintain a reasonable balance if she heels hard in a gust.

Boat C   Because of her flat floor and short keel this boat has little natural directional stability, relying mainly on her large spade rudder to keep her going in the right direction. The helmsman must work constantly to maintain course, especially with the wind abaft the beam. Often it is impossible for the helmsman to leave the wheel long enough to attend to a headsail sheet. The helm balance, which is beautiful in steady conditions, is likely to suddenly fly out of order because if the boat heels beyond the normal angle her tortured sections cause an eccentric boat shape to be immersed. This can cause a perfectly competent helmsman to have a real struggle on his hands and it is by no means unknown for such a boat to tack herself against his will.

This poor directional stability also means that it is necessary to maintain exactly the right sail combination with the wind forward of the beam. Too much sail and you have a mad bull on your hands. Not enough and the boat is stopped by the seas, because with her light weight she has little momentum to carry her through. A boat of type A or B can be harder pressed without drastic results. This may be of no concern to a full racing crew, but in a short-handed cruising yacht it can be a trial.

Ability to remain in one piece

Hull, rudder and rig must not fail. In the end, success depends on the boat being well found. Generally a heavier boat will have an easier motion and probably a heavier, stronger rig and fittings.

Boats A and B have properly supported rudders. If boat C were to fall backwards off a wave with her rudder hard over, the shaft would need to be exceedingly strong to guarantee avoiding damage. There is no doubt that such rudders are unnecessarily vulnerable.

Any mast that relies on running backstays for support is a potential embarrassment in heavy weather. Boat A or C may well have such arrangements, while boat B is likely to have the sort of rig shown in the illustration below, which is as near to unbustable as you can approach – if the fittings are up to their job.

Static lateral resistance

When a hull is moving well through the water its lateral resistance depends upon the efficiency of its keel and the rest of its immersed body, and is not necessarily related to its total immersed area. A modern deep-keeled yacht of type C develops more effective 'lift' than the heavy displacement type A, so its *dynamic* lateral resistance may be greater.

Unfortunately in storm conditions the time will come when you may ask the boat to stop rather than go. The situation is then reversed. Once it is stationary a hull's resistance to drift is largely proportionate to its immersed lateral area. Accordingly boat A has enormous static lateral resistance while boat C has hardly any at all. Boat B falls in between.

Yachts of type C generally have a high freeboard and therefore a lot of windage in addition to low values for

Below: Too many production cruiser-racers have bendy rigs that are ideal for competition tuning but may be vulnerable in a big storm. A less flexible, stronger rig is a much safer bet for a serious cruising boat.

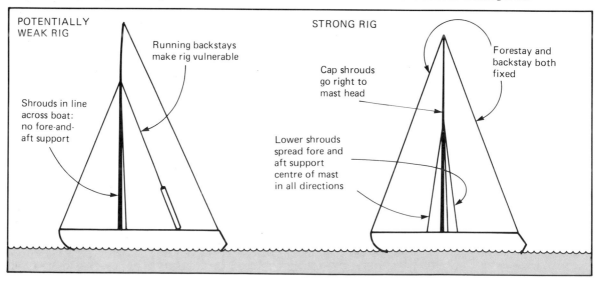

POTENTIALLY WEAK RIG

Running backstays make rig vulnerable

Shrouds in line across boat: no fore-and-aft support

STRONG RIG

Forestay and backstay both fixed

Cap shrouds go right to mast head

Lower shrouds spread fore and aft support centre of mast in all directions

static lateral resistance. Their ability to go sideways once the keel has stalled is therefore considerable.

This feature also affects handling under power at low speed in harbours in the sort of vicious cross-winds to be expected when sheltering from storms. Boat A is well-mannered and steady, boat B behaves herself, but boat C is liable to embarrass you by blowing sideways if you give her a ghost of a chance.

Motion

A lively motion will rapidly wear out all hands, leading to accidents, bad decisions, lethargy and a multiplication of sorrows.

Boat A will have an easy motion because her weight and consequent inertia resist the effect of every passing wavelet. Her gentle sections will assist and so will the fact that her mass is comparatively evenly distributed.

Boat C, with her light weight, flat bottom, low inertia and concentrated ballast will show a marked tendency to throw sleepers from their bunks, sailors off the foredeck, cooks into the soup and everyone into a tired, irritable humour.

Boat B lies somewhere between the two.

Pumpability

Any boat is capable of accidental flooding or, at least, of taking in too much water for comfort in a bad gale. If her pumps are to stand a chance of clearing her a boat must have a deep bilge for the water to drain into.

Right: A fine, sea-going cockpit; not too wide, and fitted with deep, protective coamings.
Below: A flat-floored boat with no real bilge cannot be pumped out, and will soak her accommodation.

Deep bilge:
dry bunks and
happy pumping

Shallow bilge:
wet bunks and
pump failure

Boat A has an enormous capacity to keep unwanted water below the cabin sole. Furthermore, since the water can pass straight into the bilge it will probably remain clean of debris and less likely to clog the pump strumboxes. Water has to be present in colossal quantities before it encroaches on the accommodation, food lockers, batteries and all the other items you would prefer to keep dry, and since the pump inlet is well down in the keel it should never come to this.

Boat B may well have an adequately deep bilge space. Some do, some don't.

Boat C may have virtually *no bilge at all*. The only way to keep your lockers dry on such a vessel is to sponge out the bilge, as the floor of the boat is so flat that a two-inch pump suction cannot get a grip on the bilge water until there is sufficient to invade the accommodation. It would be a pleasure to watch the designer of such a boat sponging out his once spotless bilge, now slopping with all the usual joys, during his watch below in a midnight gale.

A secure helming position

All boats, whatever their type, must have a steering position that is comfortable and secure. This means that the cockpit must be deep and low down in the boat. It is not insignificant that all Bristol Channel Pilot Cutters had deep, self-draining cockpits sited right aft. These boats were conceived by men of vast experience to be safe at sea. Walk-through accommodations, aft staterooms big

Above: A poor cockpit design. The section forward of the wheel may be safe enough but the aft area would be a dangerous place to linger in a big sea.

enough for a multiple orgy, and other such considerations came nowhere in their planning. They were concerned only with producing the most seaworthy arrangement possible, and they knew what they were doing.

Many modern yachts have excellent cockpits the pilots would have enjoyed, but to perch a shallow dish up on the top of the midships' accommodation, call it a 'centre cockpit' and invite honest yachtsmen to risk their lives there in a steep breaking sea is the height of irresponsibility, or ignorance, or both.

Capacity to anchor successfully

Anchoring may be the last card in your hand that will save you from stranding, but even if you are merely riding out a gale in a sheltered anchorage you need a well-mannered boat if you do not want to be up half the night dragging, or in fear of dragging.

Boat A, because of her great inertia and static lateral resistance, will not sheer about a great deal when lying to anchor. Her comparatively deep forefoot will help as well. Furthermore, since she is heavy, carrying the extra weight of plenty of good ground tackle will not be a problem for her – so she has no excuse for not being suitably equipped. Also, her low freeboard will keep down her hull windage. All of which will give her anchors the best change of holding firm

Boat B has less forefoot and is lighter for her length, so she will not lie so quietly.

Boat C will allow her head to blow off with every gust of wind. She will sail around shamelessly, snubbing her anchor at the end of each surge. Even if she doesn't pull it out, her ill-mannered behaviour will not encourage confident slumber.

Stability

Given that the skipper has arranged to keep his boat well clear of shore-related dangers, by far the greatest evil that can befall her out at sea is to be knocked down onto her beam ends, or even completely capsized. For our purposes we can think of stability as the boat's ability to resist these horrors or, if she should succumb, her power to get back on her feet as quickly as possible.

Heavy weather stability can be considered at two levels: static and dynamic.

Static stability

This is the calculated power of a boat to resist a capsizing force applied steadily, in theoretical conditions. The results by no means tell the whole story. They are, however, a good starting point.

Illustrated is a 'GZ' curve, which is a graph of the increase or decrease in a boat's 'righting arm' with changing angles of heel. The righting arm is the lateral distance between the centre of gravity and the centre of buoyancy. Depending upon the relative positions of the two centres, and how the centre of buoyancy moves with the angle of heel the boat will, at some stage, become negatively stable, which means that she will be perfectly happy to float upside down.

The two GZ curves plotted here are based on the official report on the disastrous 1979 Fastnet Race. One is for a 32-foot cruiser-racer similar to our boat B. The other is for an out-and-out racing boat of similar length overall, displaying many characteristics copied in beamy modern cruisers of type C. You will notice that boat B is extremely stable at 80 degrees of heel (virtually on her beam ends) while the flat-bottomed beamy racer is already losing stability from 55 degrees onwards.

Look at the situation at 90 degrees of heel. The righting arm of boat B is more than double that of the racer, which means that not only will she be trying twice as hard to pull herself vertical again if she is laid flat, but also that she will try twice as hard not to be pushed over in the first place!

The racing boat becomes negatively stable at about 115 degrees while our heroine fights it out right up to 155 degrees, even then, she is only marginally stable upside-down. The merest ripple would knock her back into a positively stable state. In contrast the racing boat is remarkably stable once well and truly inverted. Such craft are on record as having remained thus for minutes on end following a capsize at sea.

A heavy displacement yacht of type A has a centre of gravity which is higher than that of a fin-and-skeg cruiser/racer and her static stability probably will fall somewhere between that of the two types discussed.

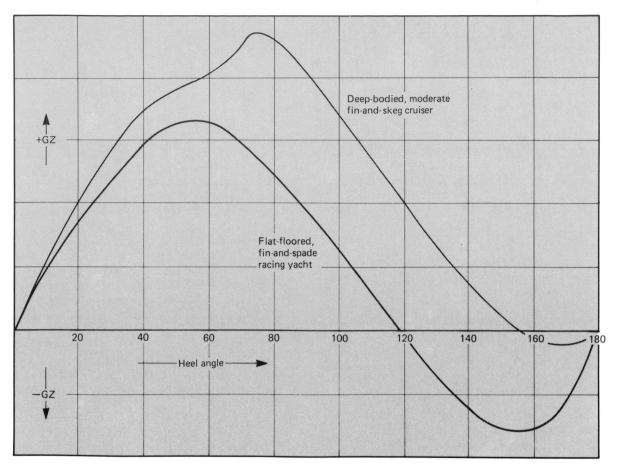

Deep-bodied, moderate fin-and-skeg cruiser

Flat-floored, fin-and-spade racing yacht

+GZ

—GZ

←— Heel angle —→

20 40 60 80 100 120 140 160 180

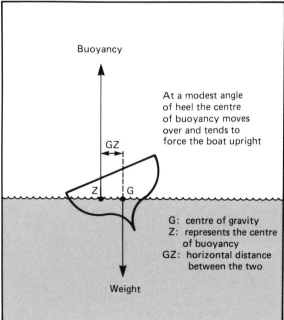

Buoyancy

At a modest angle of heel the centre of buoyancy moves over and tends to force the boat upright

GZ

Z   G

G: centre of gravity
Z: represents the centre of buoyancy
GZ: horizontal distance between the two

Weight

Above: Two GZ curves – one for a seaworthy 32-foot cruiser-racer, and one for an out-and-out racing boat. Left: The GZ curve plots the distance between the centre of buoyancy and the centre of gravity at increasing angles of heel.

Dynamic stability

When it comes to real-life situations a yacht is not hove down by a steady force: she is knocked over by wave action. Part of her capacity to resist knockdowns is expressed by the GZ curve, but there are other factors of even greater importance to consider.

Following the 1979 Fastnet Race, the Society of Naval Architects and Marine Engineers (SNAME) and the United States Yacht Racing Union (USYRU) produced a report which defined the factors which enable a yacht to resist being capsized by a breaking wave. In order to do this they drew on existing data and also commissioned a series of carefully controlled experiments.

The results of their work show that the factors which contribute most to a vessel's resistance to capsize are displacement and roll moment of inertia.

When a boat capsizes she rolls over. Rolling is a form of motion and, like any other motion, before it can get underway, it must first overcome the forces of inertia. 'Roll moment of inertia' is a convenient way of expressing the amount of inertia to be overcome before a boat begins to roll over convincingly.

The vertical position of the centre of gravity makes surprisingly little theoretical difference, though the report says that in practice 'low positions resist capsize and help assure recovery from upside down stable equilibrium'.

The elements that make up a boat's total displacement can be expressed in terms of their relative weight by this diagram for a typical yacht:

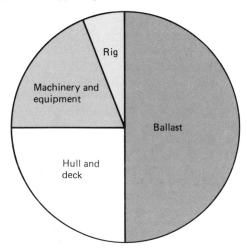

If we now express the same elements in the proportion that they affect roll moment of inertia the diagram looks like this:

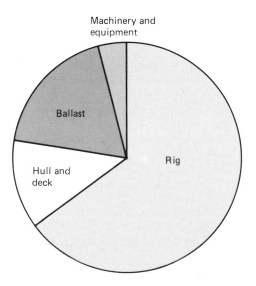

The message is clear. Contrary to what one might expect, when it comes to being capsized by a breaking wave the effect of a heavy rig is beneficial. This is because of its inertia, or its initial resistance to movement. If you hold the boat on her beam ends, a heavy rig will have a bad effect upon her GZ curve, but this is not what happens at sea. A wave hits the boat and passes on. If the boat's displacement and roll moment of inertia are sufficient to resist it, it will pass on before it has a chance to flatten her. But if the boat is light, and the weight of her rig and other factors do not give her enough roll moment of inertia, she may capsize.

Once a boat is on, or beyond, her beam ends she is going to become more interested in her GZ curve, and a heavy rig will work against her. But there is no doubt that when it comes to resisting knockdown, a good solid rig is a help rather than a hindrance. Such a rig also has more chance of staying in the boat undamaged through any traumas which may befall. If you lose your rig altogether, your roll moment of inertia almost disappears and you become vulnerable in the extreme.

Conclusions

What does all this mean for boats, A, B and C?

Boat A emerges with a reasonable GZ curve, a high value for roll moment of inertia, and plenty of displacement.

Boat B has an excellent GZ curve a modest displacement, and a roll moment of inertia one could live with happily.

Boat C's GZ curve is a fearful sight. Her displacement may well have been eroded beyond safe limits in the search for sailing performance and cheap construction though her roll moment of inertia, if she is a cruising boat with a comparatively heavy rig, may be little worse than boat B.

● Boat A's resistance to capsize is best, followed by boat B. Boat C is far behind; she is much the likeliest of the three to suffer a capsize and she is also the most vulnerable when in a capsized state. ●

Other considerations

A boat's performance in rough weather may be only one of the factors to consider when deciding what sort of boat you should be sailing. Boats of type A tend to be comparatively slow in light airs, expensive to buy and do not have much room down below. Boats like our boat C are light, airy, roomy and usually sail excellently on good days. They also handle beautifully under power in the absence of crosswinds.

The world is still waiting, and will wait, for a long time yet, for the boat that is all things to all men.

9 Riding out a gale at sea

When discussing storm survival many people become dogmatic about what should and should not be done. I would suggest that there is no single answer to such a question and that your decisions should be based on an informed appraisal of what seems right for your boat and your crew on the day. The important thing is to be aware of the various options so that you can choose the best one for the conditions.

Sooner or later it happens: you are stuck with a gale at sea. The way you choose to ride it out will depend on three things:
● Your tactical situation. That is, your position relative to your destination and any land masses or other dangers.
● Your boat's capabilities.
● Your crew strength.

Tactical considerations

It is common sense that if the gale is 'going your way' and you are not short of searoom you will run with it for as long as you can. Running also happens to be one of the recognized survival techniques, so you may do yourself a double favour so long as you can carry on in safety. On the other hand, if a lee shore is too close for comfort you will need to opt for one of the techniques designed to maintain your weather gauge. In some boats it will be sufficient to heave-to, while in others this could be suicidal.

If you are well offshore, and searoom is of no consideration, and if you can no longer safely or comfortably sail your course, you will either opt for one of the *passive techniques* (where the boat looks after herself), or an *active technique* (where you look after the boat). Passive techniques include heaving-to and lying a'hull; active techniques include running off, sailing (or motor-sailing) to windward, and heaving-to under power (or sail-assisted power).

Passive techniques

When you have a weak or tired crew, or when conditions are of such severity that no-one wants to go on deck if it can be avoided, it is wonderful to be able to leave a boat to look after herself. Unfortunately not all boats can do this, as we shall see.

Heaving-to
When discussing the question of headsail changes in Chapter 4 we looked at the basic proposition of heaving-to. If a boat heaves-to well this gives her an excellent option in any weather in which she can carry canvas. The sails will steady her and she will head the seas at an average of four or five points off (45 – 55 degrees).

The easiest way to heave-to is to tack onto a tight headsail sheet as described on page 33, but if you would rather heave-to on your current tack and you don't want to bust a gut winding the headsail across to weather, then run off and pull the sail over in the reduced apparent wind, bring the boat to, and lash the helm down.

Below: By bearing away and running off it is relatively simple to heave-to on the same tack.

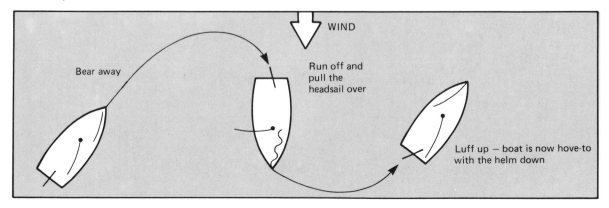

WIND

Bear away

Run off and pull the headsail over

Luff up — boat is now hove-to with the helm down

When it is time to let draw once more you can do so by simply unlashing the helm and bringing it across to windward. If the boat is well-balanced she will bear away and gybe, her mainsheet already being well in and under control. The headsail will then be on the 'right' side and off you will go. If you want to let draw on the tack on which you are hove-to, you have only to let the headsail pass across to the leeward side and sail away.

You can usually persuade a boat to go roughly where you want when she is hove-to by juggling the sheets. If you pull the jib hard up to windward and ease the main a few feet, she will stop as near dead as it is possible for her to do. Ease the jib progressively and she begins to fore-reach, moving ahead with an ever-decreasing amount of leeway as the clew of the sail comes closer to the midships position.

Some boats will fore-reach to windward with the helm left free and the jib clew pinned amidships by both sheets. Once balanced such boats will jog to weather, not pointing high, but not soaking anyone to the skin either.

Sort out what you need for your tactical situation, and what is making the boat lie as quietly as possible. When you have arranged the boat as you want her, check your drift. Use your handbearing compass to sight along the slick you are leaving. The bearing of the slick is the reciprocal of your heading. You can also make a surprisingly good estimate of the speed of your drift. Log the two figures and you'll be able to keep your plot going through the worst of the weather.

Below: Take a bearing on the slick and work out the reciprocal to find your heading. If you can estimate your drift speed you can update your plot hourly.

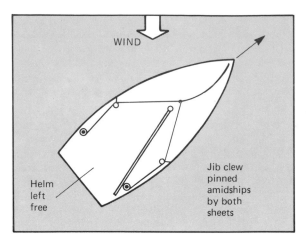

Above: Pinning the jib clew amidships using the sheets will make some boats fore-reach to windward.

Boat A heaves-to beautifully. Any time you are sick of going to windward you can put the helm down, leave the headsail where it is and take a rest. In a heavy gale such a vessel will point up well and keep her decks remarkably dry as she shoulders the seas aside. The effect down below is a dream. I once enjoyed a game of Scrabble on the saloon table of my pilot cutter while hove-to in force 9 in mid-ocean.

Such craft make little leeway hove-to; instead they tend to drift square across the wind. In a force 8 gale a 32-foot heavy displacement boat would make no more than a mile downwind in one hour. A bigger boat makes less than and this when hove-to 'dead'. Arrange for her to fore-reach a touch and you can cut the leeway down to next to nothing.

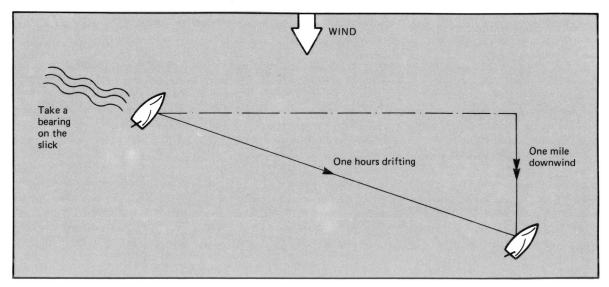

If the boat has a plumb stem like a traditional English cutter, she may lie-to satisfactorily with a staysail only – the clew amidships – and the helm lashed down. Leeway will increase a lot, but if there is too much wind to show a trisail, a double-reefed staysail alone is a halfway house before lying a'hull. A boat with a cutaway forefoot will not do this as she will lie with the wind abaft the beam and take the seas on the quarter, which is not pleasant!

Boat B will heave-to, but she will lie much further from the wind than boat A and will make more leeway – anything up to two knots in a whole gale. However, she should be safe enough unless she finds she is being knocked down heavily, because although she is tending to lie beam-on to the seas, her resistance to capsize is fairly high. But keep a close watch on developments; because if the seas grow steeper she may not be able to cope. Boats of this type fore-reach beautifully with the headsail amidships.

Boat C may not heave-to at all. Some will, but some cannot be trusted not to tack themselves as soon as you have shut the hatch. They also make a great deal of leeway, having almost no lateral resistance with the keel stalled. They generally lie beam-on or worse. Since their knockdown potential is high, heaving-to is probably not a good idea.

Lying a'hull

When a vessel is allowed to drift freely with the wind and sea, showing no canvas and not using her engine, she is said to be lying a'hull.

Sometimes a boat will heave-to under minimum canvas to ride out a gale, only to find later that the wind has increased so much that even the little sail she has left is pressing her too far down for safety. That is the time to change tactics. With a suitable boat and a crew fatigue problem you will probably decide to drag down the sails and lie a'hull.

Whether this is a good idea or not depends on the boat and steepness of the seas, but in the last resort, if the crew is sick or exhausted and it is too windy to heave-to it's a lie a'hull or nothing.

The only possible alternative is to lie to a drogue used as a sea anchor. Used in this way, however, such a device is generally agreed to be of dubious advantage. If it really does keep the ship's head to what is coming, it will impose colossal strains and also tend to hold the bow down, dissuading it from rising to steep, perhaps breaking waves. Furthermore, tremendous chafe problems are experienced where the rode passes over the stemhead. Some multihulls – which experience specialised problems in bad seas – have successfully lain passively to a type of drogue akin to a parachute, but technique is of little relevance to the monohull sailor.

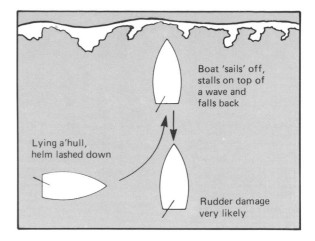

Above: The danger when lying a'hull is that the boat will sail up a wave, fall back and smash her rudder.

Given that all your deck stowage arrangements, particularly your sail lashings, are able to resist deliberate sabotage, the only job that remains before battening down is to decide what to do with the helm. Bear in mind that the boat is going to be knocked around and that, from time to time, she will gather way. If you lash the helm down to leeward (as for heaving-to) there is a possibility that she may sail herself almost head to wind up the face of a wave, fall back and damage her rudder as she plunges astern onto it. If the rudder were fixed in line with the keel it would have a better chance of surviving. On the other hand, if you lash the helm amidships the boat is not going to point up at all, so she will be permanently beam-on to what is on the menu. You see the dilemma.

The day will provide the answer, but whatever you do, lash your helm firmly. If you have a tiller, lash it not only at the end but also near the rudder stock, otherwise when you fall off a big wave the leverage of the single lashing at the forward end may allow the force acting on the rudder to break the tiller. I once had this experience, and spent the rest of the night half under water with my wife holding onto my boots as I tried to jury-rig a tiller. Not recommended for the faint and weary traveller.

Lying a'hull in a suitable boat is less uncomfortable than you might suppose. One would expect to roll frantically but this is not the case. A solid wind of force 10 or more exerts so much force on the rigging that the boat rarely rolls to windward of the upright position, but because you are lying in the trough of the waves you have to accept the possibility of some sort of a knockdown. For this reason, before deciding to lie a'hull you will need to consider whether it would be a wise move for your boat.

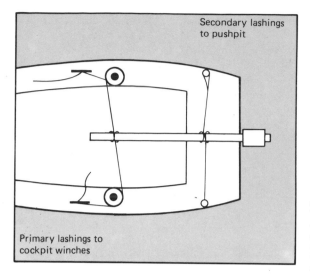

Above: To keep the tiller in one piece put two lashings on it – one at the end, and one near the rudder stock.

Boat A is heavy, has a beneficial roll moment of inertia and a reasonable GZ curve even if she should be laid over. This boat has a fair option in lying a'hull.

Boat B is lighter than boat A; she must accept the greater probability of taking a knockdown, but she has an excellent stability curve so she can expect to fight hard and to right herself if she should be unlucky.

Boat C is light and has a poor value for roll moment of inertia; she also has a lousy GZ curve indicating a fine potential for floating upside down. It would probably be best to try another tactic.

Conclusions

If you are looking for a boat that can take care of herself in heavy weather, you should consider a heavy, or moderate displacement yacht with a deep body. Light, flat-floored, beamy cruisers will require a lot of help from you if they are to come through without embarrassment.

Active techniques

It should by now be clear that there are occasions when positive measures need to be taken if you, your crew and your boat are to survive a blow unscathed. If the boat is constitutionally unable to look after herself all passive techniques must be discounted, but even when a vessel is well suited to the passive methods circumstances may dictate a preference for some active effort by her crew. Once again, we'll look at the recognized techniques and place each in the context of how suitable it may be for a particular type of yacht.

Running with the storm

The most obvious advantage of running off in heavy wind and seas is that the force of both is lessened. If you are trying to sail to windward in an apparent wind of force 10 and you turn and run off at even a sensible speed, your apparent wind drops to a friendly force 8, while the force of any breaking seas is correspondingly less as well.

The second benefit is that you present the boat at a favourable aspect to any seas with the potential to capsize her. Beam-on to the waves she is at her most vulnerable, but if she can take the seas end-on, either bow or stern, she is as safe as she can be.

Dangers of running

Pooping   A vessel is 'pooped' when a breaking wave overwhelms her from the stern. Being pooped is not to be confused with a small crest slopping over the transom and tipping a few gallons of water into the cockpit. If you are pooped, you'll know the difference. A boat can be pooped in any bad sea, but if speed is kept to a sensible level as described in the section on running in Chapter 4, the risk will be minimised. This is because if you are going too fast, you will be pulling a stern wave which will add itself to any following sea and may persuade it to break with unhappy results. Because of the danger of pooping, and also of broaching, it is *vital* to keep the main companionway battened down when running in heavy weather. If the helmsman feels lonely, tell him to sing a song, but *don't* leave that top washboard out. You may live to regret it. Or perhaps not. . .

Broaching   The dangers of broaching have been discussed in Chapter 4. They can be minimised by doing all you can to reduce rolling and by sailing at a sensible speed. The use of warps may also help, as we shall see.

Pitchpoling   Pitchpoling is what happens when a boat is running in an exceptionally high, steep sea and she is flipped stern over bow. It is an unlikely contingency outside the Southern Ocean or the North Atlantic 'out of season'. I have no experience of such a situation, but for readers who wish to know more, Bernard Moitessier gives an excellent account in his book *The Long Way*.

Special techniques for heavy weather running

The object of the exercise, remember, is to maintain a comfortable speed (see Chapter 4) and to keep steering so as to take the seas 'stern on'.

Bare poles   As the wind rises and speed gets out of hand the first thing to do is to remove the last rag of sail and continue under 'bare poles'. This works well in a heavy blow. There is no problem keeping up speed. A heavy displacement 32-footer in severe gale or storm conditions may well find herself 'sailing' at six knots without any difficulty. Try it on a windy day in calm water.

See how far off a dead run you have to come before you lose control. It's a useful exercise.

Use of warps If your speed builds up too much even under bare poles the only way to slow down is to trail something in your wake. The favourite item is a long warp towed in a bight with one end secured to each quarter of the boat. It is best to lead the warp so that it can be made fast beyond the winches; then you can use the winches to recover it when the time comes.

Two bonuses arise from slowing the boat in this way. The bight of warp will create a slick which can sometimes deter a wave from breaking; and because its fairleads are abaft the boat's turning point the rope will help the helmsman keep her stern to the seas and reduce any tendency to broach.

To be of any use at all, a warp must be towed with its bight at least one wave astern of you. If you think you will be doing this, you need a heavy rope more than 120 metres long. If you trail the dock lines the manufacturers issue with new boats, you will merely succeed in stripping off the whippings and rendering them even more useless than they already are. Every cruising boat should have one long warp for the day in harbour when nothing else will do. Here is an extra use for it.

Boat A runs well. She is not in a hurry to go too fast and with her excellent tracking characteristics she steers like a dream. If she rolls, her helm balance will not be much altered.

Boat B, being lighter than boat A, is more easily driven and will need extra care to check her speed. She will also demand more of her helmsman, but she is free of any particular vices.

Boat C will have to work hard to keep her speed down. So long as she remains level she is easy to steer with her big spade rudder. But if she develops a roll or takes on a large angle of heel she is by far the most likely of the three to overpower her helmsman and broach. This is because her flat floor and beamy shape create a highly asymmetrical hull shape at extreme heel which destroys her helm balance.

The drogue

In recent years considerable work has been done by various authoritative bodies to test the usefulness of a drogue towed astern while running in heavily breaking seas. A drogue is a recoverable device which floats just below the surface of the water and exerts a strong pull on the rope by which it is streamed from its parent vessel. In cases where the boat needs to be slowed down and her bight of streamed warp is proving inadequate for the purpose, she can deploy her drogue and achieve a far more effective result. One school of thought even suggests that a vessel can best ride out a storm by simply lying stern to such a device and securing the hatches. Her crew are recommended to sit tight down below, restrained by 'aircraft-type safety harnesses'. Perhaps these folk are right but I, for one, can't help wondering what Joshua Slocum would have made of such a theory. The idea of the Old Man happily riding out a gale strapped firmly in his bunk, out of reach of his tobacco, is hard to grasp.

Probably a more useful way to employ a drogue is that practised by many professional power-boat operators such as the RNLI (Royal National Lfeboat Institution). These men and women have found that if they stream a drogue over the stern and then motor ahead against its pull, they achieve excellent down-wind (and down-wave) control. This highly effective method could also be considered by a sailing vessel. Instead of running under bare poles she could set a storm jib to provide power and help the rudder to bite, and use the drogue to keep the speed down.

A modern drogue is not a bulky item when stowed, and owners of the type of yacht more prone to rapid drifting in high winds would be well advised to consider including one in their stores list. It is as well to remember, however, that the loads a drogue impose upon a hull are massive (up to 7,500lb for a three-foot diameter drogue!) so its proposed attachment bollard needs to be beyond suspicion of weakness. A further consideration is that during a single average storm the streaming line of a drogue is likely to ease and then take the strain 10,000 times, and it will chafe through long before the storm is over unless the most stringent preventative measures are taken.

Sailing to windward

Traditionally this would never have been considered a serious proposition as a survival technique. Modern developments in boat design, however, have made it not only possible but in some cases desirable.

For the boat which is debarred by her shape and concept from being able to look after herself, sailing to windward must be looked at as a way of riding out a moderate gale.

The benefits of sailing to windward are that the bow of the boat can be presented to a nasty sea and that, because the boat is moving at a good speed, the helmsman can go some way towards dodging the really wicked ones. Helming technique of a high calibre is essential and considerable powers of endurance are required, both from the helmsman and those around below as the yacht tries to shake herself to pieces.

A boat is required to be quick on the helm to succeed. She must luff to the crest, then bear away as it passes beneath her so as to avoid the bone- and boat-shattering impact of heavy pounding. Skill and experience will also be needed at the helm to decide how much wind to feed her, whether to sail her 'shy' or 'full and by' and when to do one or the other.

Clearly only a powerful yacht with superbly cut sails and bullet-proof gear can hope to execute such performance. Should you have a roller-reefing headsail 'without the option' you can discount this technique altogether, because long before these sort of conditions are reached it will have demonstrated its ultimate worth.

If your headsails aren't up to the job, you still can motorsail to windward. Take in your headsail altogether and motorsail with a deep-reefed main or trisail.

Boat A is not going to be seriously interested in sailing to windward to survive a gale in open water. She doesn't need to because she can heave-to, saving herself and her crew from a dangerously violent experience. If she were ever in the position of having to do this, she would suffer from being slow on the helm. On the other hand, her comparatively heavy displacement makes pounding a rarity.

Boats of type B are on record as having survived storms by using this technique. If such a boat is taking a bad pasting hove-to it could well be the best thing for her to do, if she doesn't care to go a-running.

Boat C can also make good use of this technique. We have seen that she really needs to keep her head up. Here is a possible way for her to do so.

It cannot be overstressed that this technique is brutally hard on boat and crew. It also requires little imagination to see that sooner or later there may be too much wind to carry on.

Heaving-to under sail-assisted power

One of the favourite survival tricks in a displacement motor yacht is to heave-to under power. The boat is headed into the weather and her throttles are set so as to maintain steerage way, or a touch more.

Nowadays most sailing yachts have powerful auxiliary engines. Maybe not powerful enough to heave-to under engine alone, but if the mainsail or trisail is left setting, sheeted hard amidships, and the engine used to maintain the boat at 20 degrees or 30 degrees from what is coming, you have another survival system which when all else fails may be a saviour.

Any of our three types of boat might care to make use of this, but how effective it is will depend on the engine and the type and siting of the propellor. For boat C, particularly if she is small and has a poor suit of sails, the method may prove to be of great importance.

General remarks

No matter what shape a boat is there is no argument about the fact that, all other things being equal, the bigger she is the safer she will be. Nonetheless tiny vessels have made some remarkable voyages on the ping pong ball principle – that so long as watertight integrity is unbreached, and no bones or spars are broken, all will be well. This is a point of view.

There is a priority today (a natural priority considering the direction taken by yacht design) to pay attention to ensuring that everything will stay put in the event of a knockdown. No-one in his right mind would quarrel with this, but how much happier would we be if our boats were of a type unlikely to be knocked down in the first place.

Each owner must ask himself what his true requirements are when he or she is selecting a boat, and the answers must be honest.

A well-found yacht of sensible design and construction should be able to enjoy year after year of cruising without drama. A skipper and crew who continue to temper boldness with a sound, seamanlike approach will give her all the chance she needs to prove herself fit for the sea. Between them they will be able to take in their stride whatever the weather brings, indeed it will be their pride to do so.

It is the ability, bred by necessity, to solve their own problems that has set seamen apart down the ages. Self-sufficiency has always been their corner-stone, and today's yachtsmen must carry that legacy with an increasing sense of responsibility because as communications improve it is becoming easier every year to cry for outside assistance as soon as something goes amiss.

The sea is not a playground. It is a hostile environment whose sphere man enters at his peril. If we choose to use it for our recreation, we should treat it with the respect that is, and always will be, its proper due.